"Nothing would have t
the words of the title in the right order. We are studying
John Stott, not just reading John Stott on the Bible. For in his preaching
as in his writing, John Stott's greatest gift was to help people see and
hear clearly what the Bible itself actually says, and then, of course, to
challenge us as to how we should respond to what we see and hear. Not
all of us possess the complete works of John Stott. But we do possess
the complete Bible. These sensitively edited extracts from Stott's
writings will not only introduce new readers to the riches of his biblical
exposition (and make them hungry for more), but will surely also introduce them to riches of God's word they had not seen before."

Christopher J. H. Wright, international ministries director,
Langham Partnership

"No one I have known has loved, preached, taught and lived the Bible
any more than John Stott. He often quoted Spurgeon's comment that
we should seek for our very blood to become 'Bibline'; so seriously
should we soak in Scripture in order to know and live it. This new series
will give us daily help in just such living."

Mark Labberton, president, Fuller Theological Seminary, author of *Called*

"More than any other author, John Stott urges us to engage in double
listening. He wants us to listen to the Word God spoke and the world
God loves so that we apply the timeless truths of Scripture to the ever-
changing context of our life. To help us, he explains the Bible with
clarity, charity and humility. His writings propel us to Jesus and into
the mission of God in the world."

Greg Jao, vice president and director of campus engagement,
InterVarsity Christian Fellowship

READING THE BIBLE WITH JOHN STOTT

READING
THE SERMON
ON THE MOUNT

with

JOHN STOTT

8 WEEKS FOR INDIVIDUALS OR GROUPS

JOHN STOTT

with DOUGLAS CONNELLY

IVP Connect

An imprint of InterVarsity Press
Downers Grove, Illinois

InterVarsity Press
P.O. Box 1400, Downers Grove, IL 60515-1426
ivpress.com
email@ivpress.com

This volume is abridged and edited from The Message of the Sermon on the Mount *©1978 by John R. W. Stott, originally published under the title* Christian Counter-Culture, *by permission of Inter-Varsity Press, England. Some of the discussion questions are from* The Beatitudes: Developing Spiritual Character *©1998 by John R. W. Stott with Dale and Sandy Larsen, originally published by InterVarsity Press, Downers Grove, Illinois, USA.*

InterVarsity Press® is the book-publishing division of InterVarsity Christian Fellowship/USA®, a movement of students and faculty active on campus at hundreds of universities, colleges and schools of nursing in the United States of America, and a member movement of the International Fellowship of Evangelical Students. For information about local and regional activities, visit intervarsity.org.

Cover design: Cindy Kiple
Interior design: Beth McGill
Images: © fototrips/iStockphoto

ISBN 978-0-8308-3193-7 (print)
ISBN 978-0-8308-9334-8 (digital)

Printed in the United States of America ∞

Library of Congress Cataloging-in-Publication Data
Names: Stott, John R. W., author. | Stott, John R. W. Christian counter culture.
Title: Reading the Sermon on the Mount with John Stott : with questions for groups or individuals / John Stott, with Douglas Connelly.
Description: Downers Grove : InterVarsity Press, 2016. | Series: Reading the Bible with John Stott | "This volume is abridged and edited from The Message of the Sermon on the Mount "1978 by John R. W. Stott, originally published under the title Christian Counter-Culture by permission of InterVarsity Press, England. Some of the discussion questions are from The Beatitudes: Developing Spiritual Character "1998 by John R. W. Stott originally published by InterVarsity Press, Downers Grove, Illinois, USA." | Includes bibliographical references.
Identifiers: LCCN 2016010696 (print) | LCCN 2016011634 (ebook) | ISBN 9780830831937 (pbk. : alk. paper) | ISBN 9780830893348 (eBook)
Subjects: LCSH: Sermon on the mount.
Classification: LCC BT380.3 .S76 2016 (print) | LCC BT380.3 (ebook) | DDC 226.9/06--dc23
LC record available at http://lccn.loc.gov/2016010696

| **P** | 21 | 20 | 19 | 18 | 17 | 16 | 15 | 14 | 13 | 12 | 11 | 10 | 9 | 8 | 7 | 6 | 5 | 4 | 3 | 2 |
| **Y** | 34 | 33 | 32 | 31 | 30 | 29 | 28 | 27 | 26 | 25 | 24 | 23 | 22 | 21 | | | | | | | |

Contents

How to Read the Bible with John Stott 7

Introduction 11

   1 Matthew 5:1-6:
   Developing Spiritual Character 14

   Discussion Guide 24

   2 Matthew 5:7-16: A Christian's Influence 26

   Discussion Guide 35

   3 Matthew 5:17-30: A Christian's Righteousness . . 37

   Discussion Guide 48

   4 Matthew 5:31-48: Marriage, Truthfulness,
   Revenge and Love 50

   Discussion Guide 61

   5 Matthew 6:1-18: A Christian's Religion 63

   Discussion Guide 74

   6 Matthew 6:19-34: A Christian's Ambition 76

   Discussion Guide 87

   7 Matthew 7:1-12: A Christian's Relationships . . . 89

   Discussion Guide 99

   8 Matthew 7:13-29: A Christian's Commitment . . 101

   Discussion Guide 112

Guidelines for Leaders 115

How to Read the Bible
with John Stott

❦

During his life (1921–2011) John Stott was one of the world's master Bible teachers. Christians on every continent heard and read John Stott's exposition of Scripture, which was at once instructive and inspiring. With over eight million copies of his more than fifty books sold in dozens of languages, it is not surprising that *Time* magazine recognized him in 2005 as one of the "100 Most Influential People in the World" and *Christianity Today* called him "evangelicalism's premier teacher and preacher." At the core of his ministry was the Bible and his beloved Bible Speaks Today series, which he originated as New Testament series editor. He himself contributed several volumes to the series, which have now been edited for this Reading the Bible with John Stott series.

The purpose of this volume is to offer excerpts of Stott's *The Message of the Sermon on the Mount* in brief readings, suitable for daily use. Though Stott was himself an able scholar, this series avoids technicalities and scholarly debates, with each reading emphasizing the substance, significance and application of the text.

Following each set of six readings is a discussion guide. This can be used by individuals to help them dig more deeply into the text. It can also be used by study groups meeting regularly. Individuals in the groups can go through the six readings between group meetings and then use the discussion guide to help the group understand and apply the Scripture passage. Discussions are designed to last between forty-five and sixty minutes. Guidelines for leaders at the end of this volume offer many helpful suggestions for having a successful meeting.

If you are a group member, you can help everyone present in the following ways:

1. Read and pray through the readings before you meet.

2. Be willing to participate in the discussion. The leader won't be lecturing. Instead all will be asked to discuss what they have learned.

3. Stick to the topic being discussed and focus on the particular passage of Scripture. Only rarely should you refer to other portions of the Bible or outside sources. This will allow everyone to participate on equal footing.

4. Listen attentively to what others have to say. Be careful not to talk too much but encourage a balanced discussion among all participants. You may be surprised by what you can learn from others. Generally, questions do not have one right answer but are intended to explore various dimensions of the text.

5. Expect God to teach you through the passage and through what others have to say.

6. Use the following guidelines and read them at the start of the first session.

- We will make the group a safe place by keeping confidential what is said in the group about personal matters.

- We will provide time for each person to talk who wants to.

- We will listen attentively to each other.

- We will talk about ourselves and our own situations, avoiding conversation about others.

- We will be cautious about giving advice to one another.

John Stott had an immense impact on the church in the last half of the twentieth century. With these volumes readers today can continue to benefit from the riches of the Bible that Stott opened to millions.

Introduction

The Sermon on the Mount is probably the best-known part of the teaching of Jesus, though arguably it is the least understood, and certainly it is the least obeyed. It is the nearest thing to a manifesto that he ever uttered, for it is his own description of what he wanted his followers to be and to do.

The Sermon is found in Matthew's Gospel toward the beginning of Jesus' public ministry. Immediately after his baptism and temptation in the wilderness, Jesus had begun to announce the good news that the long-promised kingdom of God was on the threshold. He had come, in fact, to inaugurate it. With him the new age had dawned, and the rule of God had broken into history. "Repent," Jesus cried, "for the kingdom of heaven has come near" (Matthew 4:17). Matthew adds that Jesus "went throughout Galilee, teaching in their synagogues, [and] proclaiming the good news of the kingdom" (Matthew 4:23). The Sermon on the Mount is to be read and understood in that context. It describes what human life and human community look like when they come under the gracious rule of God.

And what do they look like? Different! Jesus emphasizes in this Sermon that his true followers, the citizens of God's kingdom, are to be entirely different from others. They are not to take their cue from the people around them but from Jesus, and so prove to be genuine children of their heavenly Father. The character of Jesus' followers is to be marked by qualities that are distinct from the world. They are to shine like lights in the prevailing darkness. Their righteous deeds are to exceed the deeds even of the religious leaders, while their love is to be greater and their ambition nobler than what is displayed by their unbelieving neighbors.

The followers of Jesus are to be different—different from both the compromised church and the secular world. The Sermon on the Mount is the most complete delineation anywhere in the New Testament of the Christian counterculture. This is life in the kingdom, a fully human life lived out under God's rule.

Some people have read this Sermon and have concluded that no one can really live out the principles and commands that are written here. They conclude that the teaching in these chapters represents the unpractical idealism of a visionary. It is a dream that could never come true. At the opposite extreme are those people who glibly claim to "live by the Sermon on the Mount." When you hear someone say that, it's probably best to assume that they have never really read the Sermon!

The truth of how we are to read the Sermon is that both extremes are wrong. Jesus held up these standards as principles of kingdom living, but he also realized that much more than mere human effort was required to reach these standards. The goals of the Sermon are attainable but only by those who have experienced the new birth and who have access to the Holy Spirit's enabling power. Jesus spoke the Sermon to those who were already his disciples and citizens of God's kingdom and children in God's family. Without the transformation of the new birth, this Sermon will lead us only to foolish optimism or hopeless despair.

The Sermon on the Mount has a unique fascination. It presents the heart of the teaching of Jesus; it makes goodness attractive; it shames our shabby performances; it stirs dreams of a better world. I have to confess that I have fallen under its spell—or rather under the spell of the one who preached it. My aim in these readings is to let the Sermon speak, or better to let Jesus speak it again. It's a Sermon the church needs to hear again.

Jesus did not give us an academic treatise calculated merely to stimulate the mind. I believe he meant his Sermon to be obeyed. If Christians wholeheartedly accepted his standards and values and lived by them, we would become the radically different society that Jesus always intended us to be—and the world would see and believe.

John Stott

1

Matthew 5:1-6
Developing Spiritual Character

❧

Listening to Jesus

MATTHEW 5:1-2

¹Now when Jesus saw the crowds, he went up on a mountainside and sat down. His disciples came to him, ²and he began to teach them.

Everybody who has ever heard of Jesus of Nazareth and knows anything at all about his teaching must surely be familiar with the beatitudes, the first statements of the Sermon on the Mount. Their simplicity of word and depth of thought have attracted each new generation of Christians and students of religion from every culture. The more we explore how to respond to the challenge of these verses, the more seems to remain to be explored. Their wealth is inexhaustible. We cannot reach the bottom.

Before we are ready to consider each beatitude separately, we need to consider some general issues.

The people. The beatitudes set out the character of a Christian, a Christ-follower. These are not eight separate and distinct kinds of disciples—some who are meek, others who are merciful, still others who are called to endure persecution. They are instead eight qualities to be found in the same person—one who is meek and merciful, poor in spirit and pure in heart, mourning and hungry, peacemaker and persecuted, all at the same time.

Furthermore, those who exhibit these marks are not just an elitist group, a set of spiritual saints or church leaders who dwell above the common, everyday Christians. On the contrary, the beatitudes are Jesus' own specification of what every Christian ought to be. All these qualities are to characterize all his followers.

The qualities. Some students of the Sermon have argued that Jesus is making a statement about social justice when he talks about the poor and the hungry. They think Jesus is calling his followers to right the inequalities and injustices of the world. Jesus was certainly not indifferent to physical poverty and hunger, but the blessings of his kingdom are not primarily economic. The poverty and hunger to which Jesus refers in the beatitudes are spiritual conditions. It is "the poor *in spirit*" and "those who hunger and thirst *for righteousness*" whom Jesus blesses.

The church has always been wrong whenever it has used Jesus' blessing of those who are "poor in spirit" either to condone poverty in general or to commend the voluntary poverty of those who take a vow to renounce possessions. Jesus may call some of his followers to a life of sacrifice and even poverty, but that is not what he had in mind when he spoke God's blessing on those who see themselves as empty-handed before God's bountiful table of grace.

Happy Is the Person . . .

MATTHEW 5:1-2

> [1]Now when Jesus saw the crowds, he went up on a mountainside and sat down. His disciples came to him, [2]and he began to teach them.

One other topic that has to be addressed before we examine the beatitudes individually is the blessing that Jesus promises. Each person who exhibits the quality commended by Jesus is called "blessed." The Greek word *makarios* means "happy," so the translation of the New Testament you are reading may say, "How happy are those who are . . ." Several commentators have explained the beatitudes as Jesus' prescription for human happiness.

No one knows better than our Creator how to bring happiness to human beings. He made us and he knows how we work best. But it is seriously misleading to translate *makarios* as "happy." Happiness is subjective, while Jesus is making an objective judgment about these people. He is declaring not what they may feel on a particular occasion (happy), but what God thinks of them and what they really are: they are blessed.

The second half of the beatitude spells out the blessing enjoyed by those who exhibit these qualities. They possess the kingdom of heaven and they inherit the earth. The mourners are comforted and the hungry are satisfied. They receive mercy, they see God, they are called the children of God. Their heavenly reward is great. And all these blessings are enjoyed together. Just as the eight qualities describe every Christian, so the eight blessings are given to every Christian. It's true that the particular blessing promised in each case is appropriate to the particular quality described. At the same time it is surely not possible to inherit the kingdom of heaven without inheriting the earth, to be comforted without being satisfied or to see God without receiving his mercy.

The eight qualities together constitute the responsibilities, and the eight blessings the privileges, of being a citizen of God's kingdom. This is what the enjoyment of God's rule in our lives means.

Poverty of Spirit

MATTHEW 5:3

> [3]Blessed are the poor in spirit,
>   for theirs is the kingdom of heaven.

When we read the first beatitude against the backdrop of the Old Testament, we discover that at first to be "poor" meant to be in literal, material need. But gradually, because the needy have no refuge but God, *poverty* came to have spiritual overtones and to be identified with humble dependence on God. The poor in the Old Testament are those who are both afflicted and unable to save themselves. These are people who look to God for deliverance, while recognizing that they have no claim upon him.

Therefore, to be "poor in spirit" is to acknowledge our spiritual poverty before God. We are sinners, under the holy wrath of God, and deserving nothing but his judgment. We have nothing to offer, nothing with which to buy the favor of heaven.

To those who recognize and acknowledge their spiritual bankruptcy before God—and only to them—the kingdom of God is given. God's rule is a gift, absolutely free and completely undeserved. It has to be received with the humility and faith of a little child.

Jesus' hearers must have been stunned by this statement. Right at the beginning of the Sermon, Jesus contradicts all human judgments and expectations about the kingdom of God. The kingdom is given to the poor, not the rich; to the feeble, not the mighty; to little children humble enough to receive it, not the soldiers who would take it by force.

In Jesus' own day it was not the religious leaders and scholars who entered the kingdom of God—men and women who thought they were rich in merit before God by their meticulous keeping of the law. Nor was it the zealous nationalists who dreamed of establishing the kingdom by blood and violence. Those who entered the realm of God's gracious rule were tax collectors and prostitutes, the rejects of human society who knew they were so poor they could offer nothing and achieve nothing. All they could do was cry to God for mercy—and he heard their cry.

It's still true today: the indispensable condition of receiving the kingdom of God is to acknowledge our spiritual poverty. God still sends the rich away empty. The way up in God's kingdom is the way down.

Those Who Mourn

MATTHEW 5:4

> ⁴Blessed are those who mourn,
> for they will be comforted.

To draw attention to its startling paradox, the second beatitude could be translated "Happy are the unhappy!" How can a person feel blessed of God when their days are marked by sorrow and mourning?

It seems clear from the first beatitude that those who are promised comfort here are not primarily those who are mourning over the loss of a loved one. Jesus instead is talking to those who mourn the loss of their innocence and their righteousness. Jesus is not speaking of the sorrow of bereavement but the sorrow of repentance.

This is the second stage of spiritual blessing. It is one thing to be spiritually poor and acknowledge it; it is another to grieve and mourn over it. Confession is one thing; contrition is another.

Jesus wept over the sins of others, over the devastation of coming judgment and over a city full of people who would not receive him. How often have we wept over the evil in the world and the approaching judgment on those who refuse God's grace?

But it's not only the sins of others that should move us to tears. We have our own sins to weep over as well. How much sorrow and grief do we experience over our own failures? We evangelical Christians, by making much of grace, sometimes have made light of sin. There is not enough sorrow for sin among us. We don't sense the burden of godly grief nearly enough.

Jesus' promise is that those who mourn over their own sinfulness will be comforted by the only comfort that can relieve their distress—God's free forgiveness. The greatest of all comfort is the cleansing pronounced over every sinner who comes to God in humble confession. Isaiah declared that one of the marks of the Messiah would be his willingness to "bind up the brokenhearted" (Isaiah 61:1)—and Jesus abundantly pours the healing oil of his grace into our wounded, scarred lives.

We look forward to the day when God will wipe every tear from our eyes and his comfort will be complete. But, until then, we still mourn over the havoc of suffering and death that sin spreads over our world.

The Meek

MATTHEW 5:5

⁵Blessed are the meek,
for they will inherit the earth.

We don't relate very well to the idea of meekness. Meekness is weakness—or at least it seems that way. So what is this meekness or gentleness that brings God's blessing upon us? Meek people have a true view of themselves. They understand their spiritual poverty before God and the amazing grace that gave them a right standing with God, and because of God's mercy and blessing to them they are gentle, humble, sensitive and patient with other people.

These meek people, Jesus added, "will inherit the earth." You would expect the opposite—that meek people would get nowhere because everybody ignores them or tramples them down. It's the tough, the overbearing who succeed in the struggle in the world or the workplace; weaklings go to the wall. That's how we usually think, but in Christ's kingdom the principles that govern this world are reversed. The inheritance we receive from Jesus is not obtained by might but by meekness.

This spiritual reality has always been grasped by holy and humble people of God. In Psalm 37 (which Jesus seems to quote in this beatitude) we read:

"The meek will inherit the land
    and enjoy peace and prosperity." (v. 11)

"Those the LORD blesses will inherit the land." (v. 22)

"Hope in the LORD
    and keep his way.
He will exalt you to inherit the land." (v. 34)

The same principle operates today. The ungodly may boast and throw their weight around, but real joy and satisfaction elude them. On the other hand, those who follow Christ, even if they are deprived of much of the world's things, can enjoy and possess the earth. We live and reign with Christ even in a fallen world. Then on the day of the regeneration of all things there will be a new heaven and a new earth for us to inherit. The way of Christ is different from the way of the world, and every Christian, even if we—like the apostle Paul—have "nothing," can describe ourselves as "possessing everything" (2 Corinthians 6:10).

Those Who Are Hungry

MATTHEW 5:6

> [6]Blessed are those who hunger and thirst for
>   righteousness,
>   for they will be filled.

Christians are different from the world. The world is engrossed in the pursuit of possessions; Christians have set themselves to seek first the kingdom of God and his righteousness. We hunger and thirst for righteousness.

Righteousness in the Bible has at least three aspects: legal, moral and social. Legal righteousness is justification, a right relationship with God. Since Jesus is speaking in this Sermon to those who have already believed in him and who already belong to him, this righteousness is already their possession. We are made right with God through faith alone in Jesus alone.

Moral righteousness is right living—righteousness of character and conduct that pleases God. Not the rule-keeping righteousness of the coldly religious but the warm, inner-driven righteousness that flows from the Spirit within us. This is the righteousness we should hunger and thirst for.

Social righteousness enters into this picture too. Social righteousness seeks to bring justice and freedom from oppression and integrity into the fabric of human culture. Christians are committed to hunger for righteousness in the whole human community.

There is perhaps no greater secret of progress and growth in Christian living than a healthy, hearty spiritual appetite.

Maybe some of us are dragging along in our spiritual growth because we have lost our appetite, our longing, for the right things. Yet in this life our hunger will never be fully satisfied, nor our thirst fully quenched. We will receive the satisfaction that the beatitude promises, but our hunger is satisfied only to break out again.

Like all the qualities included in the beatitudes, hunger and thirst are perpetual characteristics of the disciples of Jesus, as perpetual as poverty of spirit, meekness and mourning. Not until we reach heaven will we "never again" be hungry and "never again" thirst, for only then will Christ our Shepherd lead us "to springs of living water" (Revelation 7:16-17).

Looking back, we can see that the first four beatitudes reveal a spiritual progression. Each step leads to the next and builds on the one before. To begin with, we are "poor in spirit," acknowledging our spiritual bankruptcy before God. Next we are to "mourn" over the cause of that spiritual poverty, our sins and the reign of sin and death in our world. Third, we are to be "meek," humble, aware of the abundance of God's grace to us and willing to show the same grace to others. Fourth, we are to "hunger and thirst for righteousness." Confession and sorrow for sin lead us to desire to see things made right.

In the last four beatitudes we turn from our attitude toward God to our attitude to our fellow human beings. The sincerity of being "pure in heart," showing mercy, seeking to be "peacemakers" and even enduring persecution all affect our relationships and actions toward others.

Matthew 5:1-6

....

DISCUSSION GUIDE

OPEN

How do you usually evaluate the spiritual maturity of Christians? What measuring sticks do you use?

STUDY

Read Matthew 5:1-6.

1. What do verses 1-2 tell us about the setting of this message and those who heard the message from Jesus' lips?

2. How does Jesus' statement in verse 3 contradict our usual idea of blessedness?

3. In what senses do we miss God's kingdom if we do not acknowledge our spiritual poverty and need?

4. What are some excuses and evasions people use to avoid taking responsibility or expressing grief over their sins?

5. How might godly mourning over sin be expressed?

6. How might the Lord make his comfort known to someone who is mourning over sin in their own life or sin's effects in the world?

7. Would you consider yourself to be a meek person? Why or why not?

8. How do the hunger and thirst for righteousness resemble physical hunger and thirst?

9. Even though Jesus promised that we would be filled, why do we continue to hunger and thirst after inner righteousness and even social righteousness?

APPLY

1. Usually we are very aware of our own failings and dependence on the Lord. In what areas do you readily acknowledge your need of God?

2. Ask the Lord to show you relationships or situations in which you are being proud or harsh instead of gentle and humble. How can you bring the quality of meekness into those circumstances?

3. Would you say your appetite for righteousness is sharp or dull? Explain.

which of these do you identify with the most?

2

Matthew 5:7-16
A Christian's Influence

❧

The Merciful

MATTHEW 5:7

⁷Blessed are the merciful,
for they will be shown mercy.

Mercy is compassion for people in need. Jesus is not specific about which people he has in mind whom his disciples are to show mercy to. He gives no indication whether he is thinking primarily of those overcome by disaster; or of the hungry, the sick and the outcast; or of those who wrong us. There was no need for Jesus to elaborate. Our God is a merciful God who shows mercy continuously; the citizens of his kingdom must show mercy too.

Of course the world in general is unmerciful. The world prefers to insulate itself against the pains and calamities of other people. It finds revenge delicious and forgiveness tame. But those who show mercy receive it. This is not because we earn

God's mercy by showing mercy to others but because we cannot receive the mercy of God unless we repent, and we cannot claim to have repented of *our* sins if we are unmerciful toward the sins of *others*.

Nothing moves us to forgive like the amazing knowledge that we have been forgiven ourselves. Nothing proves more clearly that we have been forgiven than our own readiness to forgive. To forgive and to be forgiven, to show mercy and to receive mercy: these belong indissolubly together. Or in the context of the beatitudes, the meek are also the merciful. For to be meek is to acknowledge to others that *we* are sinners; to be merciful is to have compassion on others, for *they* like we are sinners too.

The Pure in Heart

MATTHEW 5:8

⁸Blessed are the pure in heart,
   for they will see God.

The primary meaning of the phrase "pure in heart" concerns sincerity. It means that in our relationships with both God and others we are free from falsehood. Our whole life, public and private, is transparent. Everything about us, including our thoughts and motives, is pure, unmixed with anything devious or underhanded. Hypocrisy and deceit find no place in us; we are "utterly sincere" (Phillips).

But how few of us live a genuine, open life! We are tempted to wear a different mask and play a different role according to each occasion. We are play-acting, which is the essence of hypocrisy. Some people weave such a tissue of lies around themselves that they can no longer tell which part of them is real and which is false. Jesus was the only person to be absolutely pure in heart.

Only the pure in heart will see God, see him now with the eyes of faith and see his glory in the future. Only the completely sincere can bear the dazzling vision in whose light the darkness of deceit vanishes and by whose fire all secrets are uncovered.

The Peacemakers

MATTHEW 5:9

⁹Blessed are the peacemakers,
  for they will be called children of God.

Every Christian, according to this beatitude, is called to be a peacemaker both in the community and in the church. Jesus made it clear that we should never seek conflict or be responsible for it. On the contrary, we are called to peace; we are actively to pursue peace; and so far as it depends on us, we are to live at peace with all those around us.

Peacemaking is a divine work. Peace means reconciliation, and God is the author of both peace and reconciliation. The very same word used in this beatitude of us is applied by the apostle Paul to what God has done through Jesus Christ. Through Christ, God was pleased "to reconcile to himself all things, . . . making peace through his blood, shed on the cross" (Colossians 1:20). It is hardly surprising, then, that the particular blessing attached to peacemakers is that "they will be called children of

God." They are seeking to do what their Father has done, loving the people he loves. God loves reconciliation, and he is now doing through his children the same thing he was doing through his Son—making peace.

It's important to remember, however, that God's peace is not appeasement; it's not peace at any price. He made peace with us at immense cost, at the price of the life-blood of his only Son. We too (though in our lesser ways) will find peacemaking a costly endeavor. Struggling to reconcile two individuals or two groups who are at odds with one another can be challenging. The time and energy to listen well to both sides is costly, as is ridding ourselves of prejudice, of striving to understand opposing points of view and of risking misunderstanding, ingratitude or failure.

peace making isnt always peaceful

When we are personally involved in a dispute or disagreement, there will be either the pain of apologizing to the person we have injured or the pain of freely forgiving the person who has injured us. Of course a cheap peace can be bought by cheap forgiveness. But true peace and true forgiveness are costly treasures.

Those Who Are Persecuted

MATTHEW 5:10-12

> [10]Blessed are those who are persecuted because of
> righteousness,
>> for theirs is the kingdom of heaven.

> [11]Blessed are you when people insult you, persecute you
> and falsely say all kinds of evil against you because of me.
> [12]Rejoice and be glad, because great is your reward in

heaven, for in the same way they persecuted the prophets
who were before you.

It may seem strange that Jesus passes directly from peacemaking
to persecution, but the reality is that as hard as we may try to
live at peace with some people, they may refuse to live at peace
with us. Not all attempts at reconciliation succeed. A few people
may even take the initiative to insult us or formulate all kinds of
evil against us. This doesn't happen because of our appearance
or our ethnic background but "because of righteousness" and
because we associate with Jesus. Some people find distasteful the
very righteousness we hunger and thirst for. They have rejected
the Master we seek to follow, and they take it out on us.

How does Jesus expect his disciples to react under persecution?
We are to rejoice and be glad! Not retaliate, not sulk, not complain,
not run away. We are to rejoice. We respond like that for several
reasons. First, because Jesus went on to say that our reward in
heaven will be great when we endure persecution. We may lose
everything on earth, but we will inherit everything in heaven. We
rejoice also because persecution is a token of genuineness, a cer-
tificate of Christian authenticity. If we are persecuted today, we
belong to a noble succession—"for in the same way they persecuted the prophets who were before you." But the main reason we
can rejoice in persecution is because we are suffering "because of
me." We may find ourselves persecuted simply because of our
loyalty to Jesus and to his standards of truth and righteousness.

Suffering is the badge of true discipleship. The disciple is not
above his master. Following Christ means suffering, because we
have to suffer.

The beatitudes paint a comprehensive portrait of who Christians are to be. We see them first alone on their knees before God, admitting their spiritual poverty and mourning over it. This makes them meek or gentle in all their relationships. Christians don't just give in to their sinfulness, however. They hunger and thirst for righteousness, longing to grow in grace and in goodness. We see Christians next with others, out in the human community. They do not withdraw from society or insulate themselves from the world's pain. On the contrary, they show mercy to those battered by adversity and sin. They are transparently sincere in all their dealings and seek to play a constructive role as peacemakers. Yet sometimes they are not thanked for their efforts but instead are opposed, slandered and insulted on account of the righteousness for which they stand and the Christ with whom they are identified.

Such are the men and women who are "blessed," that is, who have the approval of God and finds genuine fulfillment as human beings.

Salt of the Earth

MATTHEW 5:13

> [13]You are the salt of the earth. But if the salt loses its saltiness, how can it be made salty again? It is no longer good for anything, except to be thrown out and trampled underfoot.

If the beatitudes describe the essential character of disciples of Jesus, the salt and light metaphors indicate their influence for good in the world. But the salt and light sayings also raise serious questions. What possible influence can the people described in the beatitudes exert in this hard, tough world? What lasting good can the poor and meek, the mourners and the merciful do? Won't they simply be overwhelmed by the flood of violence and evil? Isn't this small minority of radical followers of Jesus just too feeble to accomplish anything for good?

Jesus did not tolerate any such skepticism; he believed the exact opposite. The world will undoubtedly persecute the church, but it is the church's calling to serve this persecuting world. To demonstrate how Christians can influence the world, Jesus used two household metaphors. Every home, however poor, used both salt and light. During his own boyhood Jesus must have often watched his mother use salt in the kitchen and light the lamps when the sun went down. Salt and light are indispensable household commodities.

The salt saying is not difficult to understand: "You are the salt of the earth." The world decays like rotten fish or meat, while the Christian presence in society hinders that decay. God intends the most powerful restraining influence to be his own redeemed, regenerate and righteous people.

The effectiveness of that salt is conditional, however; it must retain its saltiness. Strictly speaking, salt never loses its saltiness. Sodium chloride is a very stable chemical. It only loses its saltiness when it becomes mixed with impurities. It may appear to be a white, granulated substance, but it is so contaminated that it becomes useless. It is just road dust.

Christian saltiness is Christian character as it is depicted in the beatitudes—following hard after Jesus. If Christians become contaminated by the impurities of the world, however, they lose their ability to preserve or restrain anything. They may look like Christians, but their influence for good is gone. If we Christians are indistinguishable from the non-Christians, we are useless. We might as well be discarded like saltless salt.

The Light of the World

MATTHEW 5:14-16

> [14]You are the light of the world. A town built on a hill cannot be hidden. [15]Neither do people light a lamp and put it under a bowl. Instead they put it on its stand, and it gives light to everyone in the house. [16]In the same way, let your light shine before others, that they may see your good deeds and glorify your Father in heaven.

Jesus' second affirmation about the influence of Christians is "you are the light of the world"—and Jesus makes clear that the light is our "good deeds." The phrase "good deeds" is a general expression that covers everything Christians say and do because they are Christians, every outward and visible mark of faith, including the testimony of their words. Since light is a common biblical symbol of truth, the shining light of Christians must surely include their spoken testimony. Evangelism must be counted as one of the good works by which our light shines and our Father is glorified. Our light is to shine, not be concealed; we are to be willing for our Christian character to be visible to all.

Good works are acts of love and faith. They express not only our loyalty to God but our care for others as well. The primary meaning of *works* must be practical, visible deeds of compassion.

When people see these, Jesus said, they will glorify God, for they embody the good news of his love that we proclaim. Without them our gospel loses its credibility and our God his honor.

So Jesus calls his disciples to exert a double influence on the community, a negative influence by arresting its decay (as salt) and a positive influence by bringing light into the darkness. God intends us to penetrate the world. Christian salt has no business to remain safe and sound inside churchy little salt-shakers. Instead we are to be rubbed into the secular world around us to stop it from going bad. When society does go bad, we Christians tend to throw up our hands and blame the evilness of our culture. But we can hardly blame unsalted meat for going bad; it can't do anything else. The real question is, where is the salt?

But human culture needs more than just barricades to stop it from becoming as bad as it can be. People in our culture need regeneration, new life through the gospel. So our second calling is to be the light of the world. The truth of the gospel is the light, contained in fragile clay lamps, yet shining brightly into the spiritual and moral darkness around us. This is the way we will be blessed, and this is the way the world will be served. This is also the way God will be glorified. Jesus tells those of us who desire to follow him that if we let our light shine so that our good works are clearly seen, our Father in heaven will be exalted.

Matthew 5:7-16

....

Discussion Guide

Open

Have you ever been insulted or attacked because of your commitment to Jesus? How did you respond to those who came against you?

Study

Read Matthew 5:7-16.

1. Describe a time when you received mercy from someone else and the difference it made in your life.

2. Think of someone you know whom you would describe as "pure in heart." What are the distinguishing marks of that person's life?

3. What are some of the costs of being a peacemaker?

4. What are some of the rewards of being a peacemaker?

5. What reasons did Jesus give us to rejoice when we are persecuted?

6. Identify some differences between being persecuted for the sake of Christ and simply drawing opposition for being obnoxious.

7. When have you seen a Christian individual or group act as salt in the community or culture?

8. What things make Christians less salty?

9. What things prevent our light as Christians from being seen?

10. Think of some ways in which you could shine more brightly in your workplace or community.

APPLY

1. Rewrite the beatitudes and insert your name in each—"Blessed is _____ when he/she is a peacemaker." Then think of specific situations where you could put the beatitudes into practice in your life. For example, to whom can you show mercy this week? In what situation can you act as an agent of peace and reconciliation?

2. Think of a social evil that you can learn more about and take a stand against—stopping human trafficking, feeding the hungry, adopting children who are orphaned. How can you act as salt in your area of influence?

3. Who else might join you or who might you join in this effort?

Matthew 5:17-30
A Christian's Righteousness

❧

Christ and the Law

MATTHEW 5:17-18

> ¹⁷Do not think that I have come to abolish the Law or the
> Prophets; I have not come to abolish them but to fulfill
> them. ¹⁸For truly I tell you, until heaven and earth dis-
> appear, not the smallest letter, not the least stroke of a pen,
> will by any means disappear from the Law until everything
> is accomplished.

Jesus begins this section of the Sermon by telling his disciples
that they should not for one moment imagine that he had
come to abolish the Old Testament or any part of it. The way
Jesus phrases the statement suggests that some people were
deeply disturbed about his perceived attitude toward the Old
Testament. Jesus loved to use a formula no ancient prophet
or contemporary scribe had ever used. He would introduce
some of his most impressive utterances with "Truly I tell you,"

speaking in his own name and with his own authority. Was he setting himself up as an authority over against the sacred law, the Word of God? So it apparently seemed to some.

People are still asking today about the relation between Jesus and Moses, the New Testament and the Old. Jesus declared plainly that he had come not to abolish the law and the prophets, setting them aside in some way, but to fulfill them. The Old Testament contains several kinds of teaching, and Jesus relates differently to each kind, but the word *fulfilled* covers them all.

The Old Testament contains, for example, *doctrinal teaching*, instruction about God and humanity and salvation. All the great biblical doctrines are there, but it was only a partial revelation. Jesus fulfilled it all in the sense of bringing it to completion by his person, his teaching and his work.

We also find *predictive prophecy* in the Old Testament, truth that looks forward to the days of the Messiah. Jesus fulfilled it all in the sense that what was predicted came to pass in him.

The Old Testament further contains *ethical precepts* or the moral law of God. Jesus fulfilled them by obeying the moral law completely. But he went beyond personal obedience and explained what the same obedience means in the lives of his followers. Jesus' purpose was not to change the law but to reveal the full depth of meaning God intended the law to have.

This is what Jesus has to say about the law: "Truly I tell you, until heaven and earth disappear, not the smallest letter, nor the least stroke of a pen, will by any means disappear from the Law until everything is accomplished." Jesus uses the phrase "the Law" as a comprehensive term for the total revelation of the Old Testament. None of it will pass away or be discarded, he says, not a single letter or part of a letter, until it has all been fulfilled. And this fulfillment will not be complete until heaven and earth pass away. The law is as enduring as the universe.

The Christian and the Law

MATTHEW 5:19-20

[19]Therefore anyone who sets aside one of the least of these commands and teaches others accordingly will be called least in the kingdom of heaven, but whoever practices and teaches these commands will be called great in the kingdom of heaven. [20]For I tell you that unless your righteousness surpasses that of the Pharisees and the teachers of the law, you will certainly not enter the kingdom of heaven.

To disregard the "least" commandment of the law in either obedience or instruction results in demotion to the status of "least" in the kingdom; greatness in God's kingdom belongs to those who are faithful in doing and teaching the whole moral law. Jesus presses a whole new view of the law on his followers. Greatness in the kingdom is measured by a righteousness that conforms to the law, but entry into the kingdom is impossible without obedience that is better (much better; the Greek expression is very emphatic) than the obedience of the Pharisees and religious teachers.

What an impossible demand! The Pharisees and the religious teachers were notorious for their meticulous obedience to the law. Right conformity to the law was the passion of their lives. These are the people who had counted up the 248 commands and 365 prohibitions of the law and who aspired to keep them all. How can our righteousness surpass the righteousness of these supersaints, and how can this demand for such righteousness be made a condition of entering God's kingdom? Doesn't that teach salvation by our good works? Doesn't it contradict Jesus' first beatitude that says the kingdom belongs to the poor in spirit, not to the rich in righteous good deeds?

Jesus' statement must have astonished his listeners (as it still astonishes us today), but there is an answer to the dilemma. Christian righteousness is to surpass the righteousness of the Pharisees in kind rather than in degree. It's not a matter of counting the number of commandments we have managed to keep. Christian righteousness is greater than religious righteousness because it is deeper; it's a righteousness of the heart. Pharisees were content with outward, formal obedience; Jesus will teach us that God's demands are far more radical than that. The righteousness that pleases God is an inward righteousness of mind and motive. The Lord examines the heart.

This deep obedience is possible only in those who have been regenerated and indwelt by the Holy Spirit. This is why entrance into God's kingdom is impossible without a righteousness greater and deeper than the Pharisees. It is because such a righteousness is evidence of the new birth, and no one enters the kingdom without being born again.

Deeper Righteousness

MATTHEW 5:21-22

> [21]You have heard that it was said to the people long ago …
> [22]But I tell you …

The rest of Matthew 5 contains examples of this deeper right-eousness—six parallel paragraphs that illustrate the principle Jesus has just spoken. Each paragraph is introduced by virtually the same contrast: "You have heard that it was said … But I tell you." Many students of the Sermon on the Mount have maintained that in these paragraphs Jesus is setting himself against Moses. They think that Jesus is deliberately establishing a new morality while he contradicts and repudiates the old. In their minds Jesus' words could be read: "You know what the Old Testament says. But I am teaching something very different."

As popular as this interpretation is, I don't hesitate to say that it is mistaken. What Jesus is contradicting is not the law, but certain misinterpretations of the law promoted by the scribes and Pharisees. Far from contradicting the law, Jesus endorses it and insists on its authority. Jesus provides us with the true interpretation of the law; he tells us what God intended by the law.

In order to make obedience to the law easier, the scribes and Pharisees were restricting the commandments and extending the permissions of the law. They made the law's demands less demanding and the law's permissions more permissive. Jesus reversed both directions. He insisted that the full implications of God's commandments must be accepted without imposing any human limits.

The scribes and Pharisees, for example, were restricting the biblical commands against murder or adultery to the acts alone; Jesus extended the commands to include angry thoughts, insulting words and lustful looks. The ultra-religious people of Jesus' day restricted the command to love your neighbor to those of the same race and religion; Jesus said all people must be loved without limitations.

would Jesus agree with our interpretation?

Jesus disagreed with the Pharisees about their *interpretation* of the law, not the *authority* of the law. In the strongest possible terms Jesus asserted that the law was God's Word written, and he called his disciples to accept God's true intention behind the law. Our righteousness is to go deeper, much deeper, than the surface obedience of rule-keeping Pharisees.

Avoiding Anger

MATTHEW 5:21-22

> [21]You have heard that it was said to the people long ago, "You shall not murder, and anyone who murders will be subject to judgment." [22]But I tell you that anyone who is angry with a brother or sister will be subject to judgment. Again, anyone who says to a brother or sister, "Raca," is answerable to the court. And anyone who says, "You fool!" will be in danger of the fire of hell.

The scribes and Pharisees tried to restrict the application of the sixth commandment to the act of committing murder alone. If they didn't actually kill anyone, they believed that they had kept God's command. This apparently is what the rabbis had taught the people. But Jesus disagreed with that view. The true intention of the command was much wider and deeper according to Jesus. It included thoughts and words, deeds, anger and insult as well as murder.

Not all anger is evil. God frequently exhibits his holy wrath and even Jesus expressed anger at times. We as fallen human beings may feel righteous anger against injustice or cruelty. Jesus is referring to sinful anger, the anger of pride or hatred or revenge.

Insults are mentioned in these verses—words that "kill" and injure just as deeply as a knife. Jesus warns against calling our brother or sister *Raca* (a word meaning "empty" or "stupid"). He also tells us not to call someone a "fool." Jesus occasionally referred to the Pharisees and even his own disciples as "fools," so the meaning here seems to refer to a person's spiritual condition. The fool in the Bible is someone who says there is no God. This insult then is more like saying, "You are headed for hell!"

These angry thoughts and insulting words may never lead to the ultimate act of murder, but they are tantamount to murder in God's sight. Anger and insult are ugly symptoms of a desire to get rid of somebody who stands in our way. Our thoughts, our looks and our words all indicate that we wish that person were dead or that he or she would go to hell. Those evil wishes or words break the sixth commandment.

They also make us liable for judgment—not to the judgment of a human court, which may be too lenient, but to God's bar of justice. Whoever murders will be brought before a human court for sentencing, but whoever has hateful anger toward someone else will be brought before the living God. Insults and cursing will not expose us to the human council's judgment but to the fires of hell. Jesus was extending the nature of the penalty as well as the depth of the crime. Not only are anger and insult equivalent to murder, but the punishment is nothing less than severe judgment from God.

First Go; Then Come

MATTHEW 5:23-26

> [23]Therefore, if you are offering your gift at the altar and there remember that your brother or sister has something against you, [24]leave your gift there in front of the altar. First go and be reconciled to them; then come and offer your gift.
>
> [25]Settle matters quickly with your adversary who is taking you to court. Do it while you are still together on the way, or your adversary may hand you over to the judge, and the judge may hand you over to the officer, and you may be thrown into prison. [26]Truly I tell you, you will not get out until you have paid the last penny.

Jesus gives us more than just a warning in these verses; he also tells us how to avoid getting ourselves caught in such dreadful circumstances. If anger and insult are so serious and so dangerous, we must take action quickly if we are to avoid them. Jesus offers two illustrations, the first taken from going to the temple to offer a sacrifice to God, and the second from going to court to answer the charges of an accuser.

We might think of the illustrations this way: If you are in church, in the middle of a worship service, and you suddenly remember that your brother or sister has a complaint against you, get up and leave church and put the matter right. Don't wait until the service has ended. Seek out the person and ask for forgiveness. First go, then come. First go and be reconciled to the one you are in disagreement with, then come and offer your worship to God. *Why? Why not wait?*

Jesus explains things multiple times & multiple ways! So we understand.

The second illustration might make more sense to us if we think of it this way: If you have an unpaid debt and your creditor takes you to court to get his or her money, come to terms with the creditor quickly. Agree to a settlement out of court. Even while you are on the way to the hearing, pay the debt. Otherwise the court may decide on a harsher judgment against you. You may even find yourself in jail! Pay up and avoid the humiliation.

The pictures are different: one is taken from church, the other from the law court. One concerns a brother or sister and the other concerns an enemy. But in both cases the basic situation is the same (somebody has a grievance against us), and the basic lesson is the same (the necessity of immediate, urgent action).

If murder is a horrible crime, hateful anger and insulting words are horrible too. So is every deed, word, look or thought we use to hurt or offend a fellow human being. Never allow such a disagreement or dispute to continue or to grow. Don't delay in putting it right. Take immediate, drastic action to mend the broken relationship, to apologize for the grievance, to pay the unpaid debt, to reconcile with the offended person. This was God's intention in giving the sixth commandment. If we want to avoid committing murder in God's sight, we are called to take every possible positive step to live in peace with all—and to do it quickly!

why do you think he says to rush?

Avoiding Lust

Matthew 5:27-30

> [27]You have heard that it was said, "You shall not commit adultery." [28]But I tell you that anyone who looks at a woman lustfully has already committed adultery with her in his heart. [29]If your right eye causes you to stumble, gouge it out and throw it away. It is better for you to lose one part of your body than for your whole body to be thrown into hell. [30]And if your right hand causes you to stumble, cut it off and throw it away. It is better for you to lose one part of your body than for your whole body to go into hell.

Once again the religious teachers of Jesus' day were attempting to limit the scope of God's commandment that said, "You shall not commit adultery." In their view they and their followers kept the seventh commandment if they avoided the act of adultery. But Jesus taught differently. He affirmed that the true meaning of God's command was much wider and deeper than a simple prohibition of acts of sexual sin. Just as the prohibition of murder included hateful thoughts and insulting words, the prohibition of adultery included lustful looks and a sex-driven imagination. We can commit murder with our *words*; we can commit adultery in our *hearts*.

What is important to grasp is Jesus' linking of the eyes (looking lustfully) and the heart (committing adultery in our hearts). That relationship leads Jesus to give some very practical advice about how to maintain sexual purity—"If your right eye causes you to stumble, gouge it out and throw it away." Talk about a startling command! A few Christians down through the centuries have taken Jesus literally and have mutilated themselves to deter their eyes from sinful desires. But Jesus was not advocating literal physical self-mutilation; he was advocating a ruthless self-denial. Following Jesus means to take up a cross and to die to self. It also means rejecting sinful practices by putting them to death.

How does this apply in everyday life? Let me elaborate and paraphrase Jesus' teaching: If your eye causes you to sin because temptation comes to you through your eyes, then pluck out your eyes. That is, don't look! Behave as if you had actually plucked out your eyes and thrown them away, and were now blind and could not see what has caused you to sin in the past.

To obey this command of Jesus will involve for many of us a certain "cutting away."

We will have to eliminate certain things from our lives that either are or could become sources of temptation. If your eye causes you to sin, don't look; if your foot causes you to sin, don't go; and if your hand causes you to sin, don't do it. It is better to lose the use of one body part and enter life mutilated, Jesus said, than to retain your whole body and go to hell. Or in the view I take of this verse: It is better to forgo some experiences this life offers in order to enter into the life that is life indeed.

Of course this teaching runs counter to our modern views on permissiveness. It is based on the principles that eternity is more important than time and that any sacrifice to follow Jesus is worth it. We have to decide whether to live for this world or the next, whether to follow the crowd or Jesus.

Matthew 5:17-30

DISCUSSION GUIDE

OPEN

What is your view of the Old Testament? Do you avoid it or find it difficult—or do you enjoy and profit from reading it?

STUDY

Read Matthew 5:17–30.

1. How do you see Jesus in relation to the Old Testament?

2. How do you distinguish between the parts of the Old Testament we should still obey and the parts no longer binding on us? For example, what is the difference between the Ten Commandments and the laws regarding what animals to bring for a sacrifice to the Lord?

3. Given the enthusiasm and devotion of the scribes and Pharisees for keeping every detail of the law, how can a Christian's righteousness exceed theirs?

4. Jesus declares God's full intention in giving the law by explaining what is really involved in obeying and keeping the law. What was the focus of the scribes and Pharisees?

5. What is to be our focus in submitting to the law?

6. Do you think Jesus is forbidding all killing in verse 21? For example, what about a just war or self-defense? Explain.

7. Usually, we think murdering someone is worse than thinking of doing it. Why then in Jesus' view do hatred and insults bring the same guilt and judgment as actual murder?

8. What was the focus of the scribes and Pharisees when it came to the seventh commandment, God's prohibition of adultery?

9. How does Jesus clarify and explain God's original intent behind the commandment?

10. How would you explain the "gouge out your eye" command to another Christian?

APPLY

1. What can you do to expand your understanding and appreciation of the Old Testament?

2. What broken relationships did you think about when you read verses 23-26?

3. What might you need to do right now in the light of what Jesus says?

4. When do you struggle most deeply with sexual temptation?

5. What "cutting away" might help you avoid those temptations?

Matthew 5:31-48
Marriage, Truthfulness, Revenge and Love

❦

Faithfulness in Marriage

MATTHEW 5:31-32

> [31]It has been said, "Anyone who divorces his wife must give her a certificate of divorce." [32]But I tell you that anyone who divorces his wife, except for sexual immorality, makes her the victim of adultery, and anyone who marries a divorced woman commits adultery.

Jesus' third illustration of how God intended the law to be obeyed relates to divorce—or, more accurately, to faithfulness in our marriages. I confess that I am reluctant to talk about these verses because divorce is such a controversial and complex subject. It is also a subject that touches human emotions at their deepest level. There is almost no unhappiness so heartbreaking as the unhappiness of an unhappy marriage, and almost no tragedy as great as the deterioration of the relationship that God meant for love and fulfillment into a nonrelationship of bitterness and despair. Although

I believe that God's way in most cases is not the route of divorce, I hope I write with sensitivity and compassion. I have no wish to add to anyone's distress or pain. At the same time, I am convinced that the teaching of Jesus on this and every subject is good—good for every person and good for society.

One fact to keep in mind as we walk through this passage is that these two verses do not represent everything Jesus and the New Testament writers taught about divorce. This is a summary of what Jesus said on this occasion, not the whole story.

The popular opinion and religious teaching of the first century regarded divorce lightly; Jesus, in contrast, took divorce very seriously. He took divorce seriously because he took marriage seriously. Most rabbis, it seems, held to a view of divorce that permitted a husband to divorce his wife freely at his own pleasure. They held differing standards of what constituted an offense serious enough to grant a divorce, but most men could find an easy enough way out of the marriage contract. Jesus, however, saw marriage as a covenant and warned married men and women that, apart from one exception, divorce placed a former husband and wife and their second partners into unions that could not be described as marriages but as adultery.

Jesus' whole emphasis in debating with the religious leaders was on God's original institution of marriage as an exclusive and permanent relationship. The religious leaders were preoccupied with the grounds for divorce while Jesus focused on establishing the lasting nature of marriage. Jesus was calling his followers to love and to forgive one another and to be peacemakers in every situation of strife.

So, speaking as a Christian pastor, whenever someone asks to speak with me about divorce, I refuse to do it. I never speak with anybody about divorce until I have first spoken with them about marriage and reconciliation. It is only when a person has understood and accepted God's view of marriage and God's call to reconciliation that a possible context has been created within which we may regretfully go on to talk about divorce.

Honest Speaking

MATTHEW 5:33-37

> [33] Again, you have heard that it was said to the people long ago, "Do not break your oath, but fulfill to the Lord the vows you have made." [34] But I tell you, do not swear an oath at all: either by heaven, for it is God's throne; [35] or by the earth, for it is his footstool; or by Jerusalem, for it is the city of the Great King. [36] And do not swear by your head, for you cannot make even one hair white or black. [37] All you need to say is simply "Yes" or "No"; anything beyond this comes from the evil one.

The religious teachers were also permissive in their teaching about oaths. This is another example of trying to find ways to make it easier to obey God's commands. The Old Testament had a lot to say about vows, usually vows made to the Lord or in the Lord's name. So the Pharisees developed elaborate rules for making vows. If the oath included God's name, that promise was to be kept. But if God's name was not mentioned in the oath, if a person swore by something else, the promises could be broken without any terrible consequences. They shifted the attention of people away from the substance of the vow to the way it was made.

Jesus argued that the formula used in making a vow was totally irrelevant. It didn't really make any difference if God was mentioned or not. In fact, no matter how hard we try, we can't avoid some connection with God because the whole world is God's world. If we vow by "heaven," it is God's throne; if we vow by "earth," it is his footstool; if by "Jerusalem," it is his city. If we swear by our head, the head belongs to us in one sense but it is also God's creation and under God's control. We can't even change the natural color of a single hair!

A vow, according to Jesus, is binding no matter what words we use to formulate it. The real implication of the law is that we keep our promises. We are to be people of our word. That makes vows or oaths unnecessary. Honest people do not need to resort to oaths. Oath-making is really a pathetic confession of our own bent toward dishonesty. Christians should say what they mean and mean what they say. Our unadorned word should be enough—"yes" or "no."

↳ don't be scared to say no

An Eye for an Eye

MATTHEW 5:38-39a

> [38]You have heard that it was said, "Eye for eye, and tooth for tooth." [39]But I tell you, do not resist an evil person.

The two final illustrations of deeper righteousness have become the most admired and the most resented parts of the

Sermon. Jesus calls us to show love both to an evil person and to our enemies. Nowhere is the challenge of the Sermon greater. Nowhere is our need for the power of the Holy Spirit more obvious.

The quotation Jesus uses is straight out of the Old Testament. When the judges of Israel decided a case, they were to follow the principle of exact retribution. The punishment was to fit the crime, and the compensation extracted from the aggressor was to be an exact equivalent and no more. The law had the effect of defining justice and restraining revenge. But the Pharisees and religious teachers extended this principle from the law courts, where it belonged, to the realm of personal relationships, where it did not belong. They tried to use the biblical principle to justify an unbiblical action—personal revenge.

What Jesus will demonstrate is that, even though the principle correctly pertains to the law courts (and also to the judgment of God), it does not apply to our personal relationships. Our relationships are to be based on love, not justice. Our duty to individuals who wrong us is not retaliation but the acceptance of injustice without revenge: "Do not resist an evil person."

What exactly is Jesus asking us to do? We are instructed in Scripture to resist the devil—and we are warned not to resist God or his truth. But here we are forbidden to resist an evil person, a person who wrongs us. Jesus does not deny that the person is evil or that what the person does to us is evil. What Jesus does not allow is retaliation, payback or revenge.

Turn the Other Cheek

MATTHEW 5:39-42

> [39]But I tell you, do not resist an evil person. If anyone slaps you on the right cheek, turn to them the other cheek also. [40]And if anyone wants to sue you and take your shirt, hand over your coat as well. [41]If anyone forces you to go one mile, go with them two miles. [42]Give to the one who asks you, and do not turn away from the one who wants to borrow from you.

Jesus uses four short illustrations to reveal how the principle of nonresistance plays out in life. They are vivid snapshots drawn from different life situations. Each illustration introduces a person who seeks to injure or harm us—one by insultingly slapping us in the face, another by dragging us into court, a third by compelling us to do something for them, and the fourth by begging money from us. We can easily put ourselves into any one of those situations. How would we respond? In each of the situations Jesus says that our Christian duty is to avoid taking revenge or retaliating. We, in fact, are to allow the evil person to double the injury. If they slap us on the right cheek, we give them the left cheek to do the same.

Some Christians don't like this part of Jesus' Sermon. It makes them look like doormats, like weaklings. But Jesus is really advocating strength, not weakness. It takes incredible strength to act in love toward those who hurt us. It takes the selfless love of a person who, when injured, refuses to take personal revenge. Instead, that person will act for the highest

" power restrained "

good of the one who is doing the hitting or hurting. The injured Christian will certainly never hit back, returning evil for evil. Instead, Christians seek to return good for evil and are willing to give to the extreme—body, clothing, service, money— whatever is required by love.

A group of Christians down through the centuries of the church have tried to build a doctrine of absolute pacifism based on these verses, but we cannot take Jesus' command not to resist an evil person as an absolute prohibition of the use of all force or human authority. The New Testament teaches that the civil government is ordained by God to protect those who do good and to punish those who do evil. Jesus is not saying that no one should resist evil, just that we should not take the law into our own hands by seeking personal revenge. We absorb the injustice, and as a result we overcome evil with good.

Love Your Enemies

MATTHEW 5:43-45

> [43]You have heard that it was said, "Love your neighbor and hate your enemy." [44]But I tell you, love your enemies and pray for those who persecute you, [45]that you may be children of your Father in heaven. He causes his sun to rise on the evil and the good, and sends rain on the righteous and the unrighteous.

The declaration of the law was clear: "Love your neighbor as yourself" (Leviticus 19:18). In order the make the command easier to obey, the rabbis defined *neighbor* as a fellow Jew, a person from my own people who belongs to my race and who embraces my religion. I can do that pretty well. So if I limit who my neighbor is, I am free to hate my enemy—someone different from me. As a result the tradition was passed down that good conduct, normal behavior, was to love your neighbor and hate your enemy.

Jesus contradicted that accepted tradition by saying that his followers are to love their enemies. Our neighbor is not necessarily a member of our own race or religion. The neighbor may not have any connection to us at all. In the vocabulary of God our neighbor includes our enemy. Our neighbor in Jesus' eyes is simply a fellow human being who is in need, whose need we know and are in a position to help to some degree. Our duty to our neighbor, friend or foe, is to love them—and pray for them. Our enemy seeks our harm; we seek our enemy's good.

While intercessory prayer is an expression of the love we have for others, it is also a means to increase our love for them. It is impossible to pray for people without loving them, and impossible to go on praying for them without discovering that our love for them grows and matures. We must not, therefore, wait until we feel some love for them in our heart before praying for our enemies. We must begin to pray for them before we are conscious of loving them, and we will find our love break first into bud, then into blossom.

The great example of this, of course, was Jesus himself. Jesus prayed for his executioners while the iron spikes were being driven through his hands and feet. The verb Luke uses in his Gospel suggests that Jesus kept praying for them, kept repeating the prayer: "Father, forgive them, for they do not know what they are doing" (Luke 23:34). If the torture of crucifixion could not silence Jesus praying for his enemies, what pain or prejudice could silence our prayers?

Just as God expresses his bountiful blessing with rain and sunshine on the righteous and on the unrighteous, so we are to act in love to all those around us whether they are family or friends, neighbors or enemies. We are to love like God, not the world.

Loving Those Who Love Us

MATTHEW 5:46-48

> [46]If you love those who love you, what reward will you get? Are not even the tax collectors doing that? [47]And if you greet only your own people, what are you doing more than others? Do not even pagans do that? [48]Be perfect, therefore, as your heavenly Father is perfect.

Even people who don't believe in Jesus know how to love. Fallen people in a fallen world can still show profound depths of love—love as parents, love for a spouse, love for their family, love for friends. Even tax collectors (people with the worst reputation in Jesus' time) love those who love them. We Christians are called to love those who are impossible to love—the poor, the outcast, those who hurt us, our enemies—which is not possible without the supernatural grace of God. If we love only those who love us, we are no better than unbelievers. If we greet only our brothers and sisters from church, we are no better than the unchurched. It is not enough for Christians to *resemble* non-Christians in our love; we are to surpass them in virtue. Our righteous acts are to exceed the righteous acts of religious people. The Aramaic word Jesus may well have used meant "all-embracing." We are called to be perfect in love, that is, to love even our enemies with the merciful, the inclusive love of God.

We are to imitate our Father, not the world around us, and so "be perfect" as our heavenly Father is perfect. Some teachers have used this verse to teach the possibility of reaching a state of sinless perfection in this life. But the words of Jesus cannot be pressed into meaning that without contradicting other parts of the Sermon. He has already told us that one mark of a genuine disciple is to hunger and thirst after righteousness. In the next section Jesus will teach us to pray: "Forgive us our debts" (Matthew 6:12). These are clear indications that Jesus did not expect his followers to become morally perfect in this life. The perfection Jesus refers to relates to love, that perfect love of God that is shown even to those who do not return it.

Jesus accused the Pharisees of placing two serious restrictions on their love. They did exhibit love, but not to those who had injured them and not to those who were different from them. The same spirit is still around today; it's the spirit of revenge and of racism. The first says, "I will love nice, harmless people, but I will get even with those who wrong me." The second says, "I will love my own kind, but you can't expect me to love people who are different from me." In fact, Jesus *does* expect from his followers the very things that other people think cannot be expected from anybody.

In all six illustrations Jesus uses, it has become clear Christians are called to greater righteousness: a deeper, wider righteousness of the heart where the Holy Spirit has written God's law. It is new fruit exhibiting the newness of the tree, new life burgeoning from a new nature. So we have no liberty to try to dodge or duck the lofty demands of the law. Law-dodging is a hobby of Pharisees. Characteristic of Christians is a keen appetite for righteousness, hungering and thirsting after it continuously. And this righteousness, whether expressed in purity, honesty or charity, will show who we belong to. Our Christian calling is to imitate not the world but the Father. And it is by this imitation of him that the Christian counterculture becomes visible.

Matthew 5:31-48

....

DISCUSSION GUIDE

OPEN

Have you ever found that you had believed or been taught something from the Bible that wasn't correct or wasn't even in the Bible?

What should you do when someone says "The Bible teaches" and then quotes a verse or saying?

STUDY

Read Matthew 5:31–48.

1. What additional questions about marriage, divorce and remarriage does Jesus' teaching on divorce raise in your mind?

2. How does Jesus' teaching provide a foundation or starting point from which to try to answer those questions?

3. Does Jesus' statement about oaths prevent you from taking an oath in a courtroom? Explain both sides of the issue and where you stand.

4. The Old Testament did lay down the principle of "eye for eye, and tooth for tooth." How had the religious teachers distorted that command?

5. The world seems to applaud those who hate their enemies and who are most adept at paying back those who injure them in some way. How can you channel that desire for revenge into a way to act in love toward those who hurt you?

6. "It is not enough for Christians to *resemble* non-Christians in our love; we must surpass them in virtue." How is that possible for us as imperfect human beings?

7. What does it mean to "be perfect" as God the Father is perfect?

APPLY

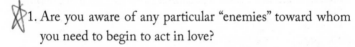

1. Are you aware of any particular "enemies" toward whom you need to begin to act in love?

2. How can you "turn the other cheek" toward someone who harasses you or seeks to harm you in some way?

3. "Jesus *does* expect from his followers the very things that other people think cannot be expected from anybody." How does this statement make you feel about following Jesus?

4. Does it challenge you—or make you want to quit? Explain.

5

Matthew 6:1-18

A Christian's Religion

❧

Parading Our Piety

MATTHEW 6:1

> ¹Be careful not to practice your righteousness in front of
> others to be seen by them. If you do, you will have no reward
> from your Father in heaven.

Jesus continues his teaching on righteousness (or living in the
right way) but the emphasis is shifted. Previously *righteousness*
referred to inner qualities like kindness, purity and honesty; now
it concerns such outward practices as giving to the needy, praying
and fasting. Jesus moves from a Christian's moral rightness to
"religious" rightness.

The fundamental warning Jesus issues is against practicing piety
before others in order "to be seen by them." At first these words
seem to contradict his earlier command to let our light shine
before others so they might see our good works (Matthew 5:16).
Now he tells us not to practice righteousness in front of others to

be seen by them. The answer to this conundrum lies in the fact that Jesus is speaking against different sins. Our human fear and cowardice makes Jesus say, "Let your light shine before others," and our human pride makes him tell us to beware of practicing our piety before others. Our good works must be public so that our light shines; our religious devotion must be secret so that we don't boast. The end result in both cases is the same: the glory of God.

Evidently Jesus expected his followers to engage in three practices: giving, prayer and fasting. He did not begin each paragraph by saying, "*If* you give, pray or fast, this is how to do it" but "*when* you do these things." Jesus took for granted that we would.

The three examples Jesus gives (pray, give, fast) follow an identical pattern. In vivid and humorous imagery Jesus paints a picture of the hypocrite's way of being religious. It's the way of pride and show. Every aspect is geared to produce the applause and attention of other people. Then Jesus contrasts the way of a follower of Jesus, which is secret, and leads to the only reward a Christian really wants—the blessing of their heavenly Father who sees in secret.

Giving to Those in Need

MATTHEW 6:2-4

> [2]So when you give to the needy, do not announce it with trumpets, as the hypocrites do in the synagogues and on the streets, to be honored by others. Truly I tell you, they have received their reward in full. [3]But when you give to the needy, do not let your left hand know what your right hand

> is doing, [4]so that your giving may be in secret. Then your
> Father, who sees what is done in secret, will reward you.

Jesus obviously expected his disciples to be generous givers, but generosity was not enough. Jesus is always concerned with motivation, with the hidden thoughts of the heart. So the question for him is not so much what the hand is doing in giving out money or gifts but what the heart is thinking while the hand is giving. There are three possibilities. Either we are seeking the praise of others, or we are quietly congratulating ourselves, or we are seeking the approval of God our Father alone.

A ravenous hunger for the praise of others was the downfall of the Pharisees and of Pharisee-like Christians today. Jesus even ridicules the way such people turn giving into a public spectacle. He pictures a pompous Pharisee on his way to church to give his offering or to take a gift to someone who is poor. In front of him march the trumpeters, blowing a fanfare as they walk, and quickly drawing a crowd. *Hypocrisy* is the word Jesus uses to characterize this performance. The word came to be applied to anybody who treats the world as a stage on which to play a part. In a movie or the theater, we expect deception. The actor or actress is playing a part and we know that. The religious hypocrite, however, deliberately sets out to deceive people. Hypocrites turn a religious practice into what it was never meant to be—a theatrical display in front of an audience. It is all done for applause.

Our Christian pharisaism is not so amusing. We may not employ a troop of trumpeters to announce every time we give, but we usually like to "blow our own horn." We draw attention to our giving in order to be praised by others.

Jesus makes the case for another way of giving, the way of secrecy. We are not to do it for the praise of others or even for our own self-exaltation. Inwardly gloating over our generosity is just as bad as bragging about it or quietly slipping it into our conversation with friends. Christian giving is to be marked by self-sacrifice and self-forgetfulness, not by self-congratulation.

Probably the only reward genuine love wants when making a gift to the needy is to see the need relieved. When the hungry are fed, the naked clothed, the sick healed, the oppressed freed and the lost saved, the love that prompted our gift is satisfied. Such love (which is God's own love expressed through us) brings with it its own private joys, and desires no other reward.

To sum up, our Christian giving is to be neither before others (waiting for the clapping to begin), nor even before ourselves (our left hand applauding our right hand's generosity), but before God, who sees our heart and rewards us with the discovery that "It is more blessed to give than to receive" (Acts 20:35).

Christian Prayer

MATTHEW 6:5-8

> [5]And when you pray, do not be like the hypocrites, for they love to pray standing in the synagogues and on the street corners to be seen by others. Truly I tell you, they have received their reward in full. [6]But when you pray, go into your room, close the door and pray to your Father, who is unseen. Then your Father, who sees what is done in secret, will reward you. [7]And when you pray, do not keep on babbling like pagans, for they think they will be heard because of

their many words. [8]Do not be like them, for your Father knows what you need before you ask him.

In his second example of religious righteousness, Jesus depicts two individuals at prayer. The hypocrite sounds fine at first: "They love to pray." But unfortunately it is not prayer they love, nor the God they claim to be praying to. Instead they love the opportunity that public praying gives them to parade themselves before others. Behind their piety lurks their pride. What they really want is applause—and they get it. "They have received their reward in full" (v. 5).

The accusation of hypocrisy has often been leveled at us churchgoers. We can go to church for the same wrongheaded reason that took the Pharisee to the synagogue: not to worship God but to gain a reputation for piety. We can boast of our private devotions in the same way. Giving praise to God, like giving to the poor, is an authentic act in its own right. An ulterior motive destroys both. It turns our service to God and others into a mean kind of self-service. Religion and charity become an exhibitionist display. How can we pretend to be praising God, when in reality we are looking for others to praise us?

How, then, should Christians pray? Jesus said, "Go into your room [and] close the door" (v. 6). We are to close the door against disturbance and distraction, but also to shut out the prying eyes of others and to shut ourselves in with God. Only with the door closed can we obey Jesus' next command: "Pray to your Father, who is unseen." Our Father is in that closed room, waiting to welcome us. Just as nothing destroys prayer like glances at who is watching us, nothing enriches prayer like a sense of the presence of God. He sees not the outward appearance only but the heart, not the one who is praying but the true motive for the prayer. The essence of Christian prayer is to seek God.

Hypocrisy is not the only sin to avoid in prayer; "babbling" or meaningless, mechanical repetition is another. The first is the problem of the Pharisee, the second is the problem of the pagan. Endless repetition degrades prayer from a real and personal approach to God to the mere recitation of empty words. Jesus is describing any and every prayer that is all words and no meaning, all lips and no mind or heart. What Jesus forbids is any kind of prayer with the mouth when the mind is not engaged.

"Do not be like them," Jesus says (v. 8). Christians do not believe in a God who is impressed by the mechanics of our prayers, and whose response to us is determined by the volume of words we use and the number of hours we spend praying. Instead we come to our Father who is not ignorant, so we do not need to inform him, nor is he hesitant to help us, so we do not need to persuade him. He is our Father—a Father who loves his children and knows all about their needs.

The Lord's Prayer—God's Priorities

MATTHEW 6:9-10

> [9]This, then, is how you should pray:
>   "Our Father in heaven,
>   hallowed be your name,
>   [10]your kingdom come,
>   your will be done,
>   on earth as it is in heaven."

The first three petitions in the Lord's Prayer express our concern for God's glory in relation to his name, his rule and his will. Jesus makes it clear that God is not some impersonal force but is "our Father in heaven"—the personal God of love and power, fully revealed by Jesus Christ, Creator of all, who cares about the creatures he has made and the children he has redeemed.

The name of God is not simply a combination of the letters G, O and D. The name stands for the One who bears it. So God's "name" is a summation of all that God is and does. His name is already holy in that it is separate from and exalted over every other name. But we pray that God's name might be *hallowed*, "treated as holy," by those who speak it. Our desire is that God's name and character might receive the honor it deserves.

The kingdom of God is God's royal rule. Just like his name, God's sovereign rule over nature and history is already a reality, but we are to pray that his kingdom will "come" in its fullness in the lives of his people and in the church and in the world. We are praying that God's kingdom will grow as people submit to Jesus as Savior and Lord, and that the kingdom will soon be seen when Jesus returns in glory to take his place as King.

The will of God is always good because it is the will of the Father who is infinite in knowledge and love. As his name is already holy and he is already King, so his will is already being done in heaven. Jesus asks us to pray that life on earth may come to more nearly reflect life in heaven.

It is easy to *say* the words of the Lord's Prayer in mindless repetition. To actually *pray* the Lord's Prayer with sincerity, however, has revolutionary implications. We are constantly under pressure to conform to the self-centeredness of secular culture. When that happens we become concerned about our own little name (liking to see it in headlines and defending it when it is attacked), about our own little empire (bossing, influencing and manipulating people to boost our ego), and about our own silly little will (always wanting our own way and getting upset when it is frustrated). But in the Christian counterculture our top priority concern is not our name, kingdom and will, but God's. Whether we can pray these petitions with integrity is a searching test of the reality and depth of our Christian profession.

The Lord's Prayer—Our Requests

MATTHEW 6:11-15

> [11]"Give us today our daily bread.
> [12]And forgive us our debts,
>   as we also have forgiven our debtors.
> [13]And lead us not into temptation,
>   but deliver us from the evil one."

[14]For if you forgive other people when they sin against you, your heavenly Father will also forgive you. [15]But if you do not forgive others their sins, your Father will not forgive your sins.

In the second half of the Lord's Prayer the main pronoun switches from "your" to "our." We turn from God's affairs to our own needs. Having expressed our burning concern for his glory, we now express our humble dependence on his grace.

Our request for daily bread should be understood as representing everything that is necessary for the preservation of life—food, health, shelter, work, family, good government and peace. Jesus was focusing on the necessities of life, not the luxuries. The petition that God will "give" us our food and other necessities does not, of course, mean that we should not work to earn the money to purchase those things. Instead, it is an expression of our dependence on God to provide for us through normal means of human labor. God's provision does not supply a month's worth of food at a time, but every day becomes an opportunity to thank God for his provision of work and life's basic needs.

Forgiveness is as indispensable to the life and health of the soul as food is for the body. So the next theme of the prayer is "Forgive us our debts." Sin is compared to a debt because it deserves to be punished. But when God forgives sin, he remits the penalty and drops the charge against us. Jesus' addition of the phrase "as we also have forgiven our debtors" does not mean that our forgiveness of others earns us the right to be forgiven. Instead it indicates that one of the evidences of being forgiven by God is our willingness to forgive those who sin against us.

The last two petitions should probably be understood as two sides to the same request: "Lead us not into temptation, but deliver us from the evil one." We could paraphrase the request like this: Do not allow us to be led into such temptation that we are overwhelmed by it, but rescue us from the schemes of the evil one. The implication is the devil is too strong for us to face alone, and we are too weak to stand against his attacks alone. But our heavenly Father will rescue us if we call upon him.

It's possible to see in these three petitions a veiled allusion to the Trinity—the Father's creation and providence provides our daily bread, the Son's atoning death provides forgiveness and the Spirit's indwelling presence provides the power to overcome the attacks of the evil one. No wonder some ancient manuscripts (but not the oldest ones) end with the doxology that proclaims God's "kingdom and power and glory forever."

Fasting

MATTHEW 6:16-18

> [16]When you fast, do not look somber as the hypocrites do, for they disfigure their faces to show others they are fasting. Truly I tell you, they have received their reward in full. [17]But when you fast, put oil on your head and wash your face, [18]so that it will not be obvious to others that you are fasting, but only to your Father, who is unseen; and your Father, who sees what is done in secret, will reward you.

Fasting, strictly speaking, is totally abstaining from food. In Scripture fasting has to do with self-denial and self-discipline. "To fast" and "to humble ourselves before God" are virtually equivalent phrases. Sometimes this was an expression of sorrow for past sin. When people were deeply distressed over the sin and guilt, they would weep and pray and fast. Even today, when the people of God are convicted of sin and moved to repentance, an appropriate sign of that humility before God is to weep and fast.

We are not to humble ourselves before God only in sorrow for past sin, however, but also in dependence on him for future mercy.

This is a special and occasional spiritual practice. Whenever we need to seek God for some particular direction or blessing, we turn aside from food and other distractions in order to seek him. One further reason for fasting is to share what we might have eaten (or its cost) with those who are hungry. God said,

> Is not this the kind of fasting I have chosen:
> > to loose the chains of injustice? ...
> Is it not to share your food with the hungry
> > and to provide the poor wanderer with shelter?
> > > (Isaiah 58:6-7)

Jesus' concern was that, as with our giving and praying so with our fasting, we should not, like the hypocrites, draw attention to ourselves. The Pharisees' practice was to look terrible and sad. It was all done so that their fasting would be seen and known and applauded by people around them. Jesus' instruction to his followers, however, was to wash their faces and brush their hair every day. On fast days they were to do it as usual so that no one looking would suspect that they were fasting. The purpose of fasting is not to advertise ourselves but to discipline ourselves, not to gain a reputation for ourselves but to express our humility before God and our concern for others in need.

In this section of the Sermon Jesus has been contrasting two kinds of piety—pharisaic and Christian. Pharisaic piety is for display, motivated by pride and rewarded only by the praise of others. Christian piety is secret, motivated by humility and rewarded by God.

Matthew 6:1-18

Discussion Guide

Open

An accusation frequently made against Christians and the church is that we are "all a bunch of hypocrites." No doubt there is some truth in that statement. How would you respond if someone said that to you?

Study

Read Matthew 6:1-18.

1. According to Jesus, what is the spiritual danger in religious activities like giving to people in need?

2. How will Jesus' instructions help you to avoid that spiritual danger?

3. Does Jesus' teaching about prayer mean that we are never to pray in public out of concern that we might have the wrong motive? Explain.

4. Can you think of examples in which Christians might babble in prayer or think they might be heard through speaking many words?

5. Why does Jesus say that his disciples should not approach prayer like that?

6. If God knows what we need before we ask him, why do we need to pray at all?

7. What do you understand by "bread" in Matthew 6:11— and why does Jesus emphasize asking God for *daily* bread?

8. Where would you most like to see God's righteous rule break out in our world?

APPLY

1. How much do the priorities of God's name, God's kingdom and God's will infiltrate your prayers? What can you do to help correct that?

2. Can you think of anyone against whom you harbor resentment or bitterness? How do you think God views that?

3. What do you think God wants you to do about resentment or bitterness?

4. Tell the group when you have fasted as a mark of repentance or for spiritual direction.

5. In what situations do you think fasting might be a proper spiritual activity in your life?

6

Matthew 6:19-34
A Christian's Ambition

❦

A Question of Treasure

MATTHEW 6:19-21

19Do not store up for yourselves treasures on earth, where moths and vermin destroy, and where thieves break in and steal. 20But store up for yourselves treasures in heaven, where moths and vermin do not destroy, and where thieves do not break in and steal. 21For where your treasure is, there your heart will be also.

In the first half of Matthew 6, Jesus describes the Christian's *private life* "in the secret place" by exploring issues of giving, praying and fasting; in the second half, he is concerned with our *public* business in the world and addresses issues of money, food, drink, clothes and ambition. God is equally concerned with both areas of life, and in both spheres Jesus issues the same call to be different—different from the hypocrisy of the religious and now different from the materialism of the irreligious. Jesus continues to place the alternatives in front of us. In these and the following verses we see two treasures (on earth and in heaven [vv. 19-21]), two spiritual conditions (light and darkness [vv. 22-21]), two masters (God and money [v. 24]) and two life purposes (our own welfare or the kingdom of God [vv. 25-34]). We cannot sit on the fence.

So first, what was Jesus prohibiting when he told us not to lay up treasure for ourselves on earth? Let's note what he was (and is) not forbidding. First, there is no ban on possessions in themselves; Scripture nowhere forbids private property. Second, "saving for a rainy day" is not forbidden to Christians, or for that matter a life-insurance policy, which is only a kind of saving by self-imposed compulsion. On the contrary, Scripture praises the ant for storing in the summer the food it will need in the winter, and declares that the believer who makes no provision for his or her family is worse than an unbeliever (Proverbs 6:6-8; 1 Timothy 5:8). Third, we are not to despise, but rather to enjoy, the good things our Creator has given us richly to enjoy (1 Timothy 4:3-4).

What Jesus forbids his followers is the *selfish* accumulation of goods, extravagant and luxurious living, hardheartedness that does not feel the colossal need of the world's underprivileged people, and the materialism that tethers our hearts to the earth. For the Sermon on the Mount repeatedly refers to the heart, and here Jesus declares that our heart always follows our treasure, whether down to earth or up to heaven (v. 21).

It ought to be easy to decide which treasure to collect, Jesus says, because treasures on earth are subject to all kinds of problems and are by nature insecure. Treasures in heaven, however, are not subject to the same destructive forces and are forever secure. The earthly treasure we so eagerly desire can be eaten away by market downturns, inflation and risky investment schemes. Treasure in heaven is unaffected by the stock market or the latest corporate profit numbers.

Treasures in heaven seems to refer to endeavors like this: the development of Christlike character (since all we can take with us to heaven is ourselves); the increase of faith, hope and love (all of which, according to 1 Corinthians 13:13, "remain"); growth in our knowledge of Christ (whom one day we shall see face to face); the active effort to introduce others to Jesus and the eternal life he offers; and the use of our resources in Christian causes (which are the only investments offering everlasting dividends). No burglar can steal these investments, and no financial crisis can make them melt away. Jesus seems to be saying: "If it's a safe investment you are after, nothing could be safer than this."

A Question of Vision

MATTHEW 6:22-23

> [22]The eye is the lamp of the body. If your eyes are healthy, your whole body will be full of light. [23]But if your eyes are unhealthy, your whole body will be full of darkness. If then the light within you is darkness, how great is that darkness!

The next contrast Jesus draws is between a blind person and a sighted person, and so between the light and darkness they each live in. "The eye is the lamp of the body." This is not literal, of course, as if the eye were a window letting light into the body, but it is a figure of speech that we quickly grasp. Almost everything the body does depends on our ability to see. We need to see in order to run, drive a car, cross a road, cook, paint, play a video game. The eye, as it were, illumines what the body does. Blind people often cope wonderfully and learn to do many things without sight, but the principle still holds true: a seeing person walks in the light, while a blind person is in darkness. And the great difference between the light and the darkness of the body is due to this small but intricate organ, the eye.

All this is factual. But it is also metaphorical. Often in Scripture the eye is equivalent to the heart. That is, to "set the heart" and to "fix the eye" on something are synonyms. One example may be enough. In Psalm 119:6, 10, we read,

> I shall not be put to shame,
>> having my eyes fixed on all your commandments. . . .
> With my whole heart I seek you;
>> do not let me stray from your commandments! (NRSV)

Similarly, here in the Sermon on the Mount, Jesus passes from the importance of having our *heart* in the right place (v. 21) to the importance of having our eye sound and healthy.

Jesus' argument seems to go like this: just as our eye affects our whole body, so our ambition (where we fix our eyes and our heart) affects our whole life. Just as a seeing eye gives light to the body, so a clear and intentional ambition to serve God and others adds meaning to life and brings light on everything we do. The opposite is also true. Just as blindness leads to darkness, so a selfish ambition simply to store up treasures for ourselves on earth will plunge us into moral and spiritual darkness. It makes us intolerant, inhuman, ruthless and greedy. It is all a question of vision. If we have physical vision, we can see what we are doing and where we are going. So too if we have spiritual vision, if our spiritual perspective is correctly adjusted, then our life is filled with purpose and drive.

A Question of Submission

MATTHEW 6:24

> [24]No one can serve two masters. Either you will hate the one and love the other, or you will be devoted to the one and despise the other. You cannot serve both God and money.

Jesus now explains that behind the choice between two treasures (where we will store them) and two visions (where we will fix our eyes) there lies the more basic choice between two masters (which one we are going to serve). It is a choice between God and money, between the living Creator and any object of our desire that we view as wealth. We simply cannot serve both.

We like to think that we can balance all of life's demands and can serve both masters at the same time—God on Sunday and money through the week, or God with half our resources and money with the other half. Jesus, however, was talking in the context of a slave and a slave master. We might be able to serve two employers, but no slave can be the property of two owners. So anyone who divides their allegiance between God and money has already given it to money. God can be served only with an entire and exclusive devotion.

When the choice is seen for what it is—a choice between Creator and creature, between the glorious God and this miserable thing called money, between worship and idolatry—it seems inconceivable that anyone could make the wrong choice. Here the question is not just of comparative durability and comparative benefit, but of comparative worth: the intrinsic worth of the One and the intrinsic worthlessness of the other.

A Question of Worry

MATTHEW 6:25-30

> [25]Therefore I tell you, do not worry about your life, what you will eat or drink; or about your body, what you will wear. Is not life more than food, and the body more than clothes? [26]Look at the birds of the air; they do not sow or reap or store away in barns, and yet your heavenly Father feeds them. Are you not much more valuable than they? [27]Can any one of you by worrying add a single hour to your life?
>
> [28]And why do you worry about clothes? See how the flowers of the field grow. They do not labor or spin. [29]Yet I tell you that not even Solomon in all his splendor was dressed like one of these. [30]If that is how God clothes the grass of the field, which is here today and tomorrow is thrown into the fire, will he not much more clothe you— you of little faith?

This passage is usually ripped away from the context and simply read as Jesus' teaching concerning worry. But don't skip the word *therefore*, which connects this teaching with what has come before. Do we want to gather wealth? Then which of the two possibilities is the more protected and long-lasting? Do we want to have purpose and confidence in following Jesus? Then what is our "eye" to be like—walking in light or walking in darkness? Do we wish to serve the best master? Which one is worthier of our devotion? It's only when we have made our choice—for heavenly treasure, for light, for God—that what Jesus says next makes sense. In other words, our basic choice of which of two masters we intend to serve will radically affect our attitude to both. We will not be anxious about the one (for we have rejected it), but concentrate our mind and energy on the other (for we have chosen him); we will refuse to become engrossed in our own concerns, but instead *seek first* the concerns of God.

Jesus' contention in this section of the Sermon is that worry is incompatible with Christian faith. Jesus calls those who anxiously worry about food and clothing "you of little faith." Jesus' argument goes something like this: God created and sustains our life. We did not make ourselves and we do not keep ourselves alive. Our life (for which God is responsible) is obviously more important than the food and drink that nourish it. Our body (for which also God is responsible) is more important than the clothing that covers and warms it. If God already takes care of the greater issues (our life and body), can't we trust him to take care of the lesser issues (food and clothing)? Just as we trust God to sustain life and to watch over our bodies, wouldn't it be sensible to trust him for less important things like food and clothes?

Jesus turns the argument around in the verses that follow. He uses birds as an illustration of God's supply of food and the flowers as an illustration of his supply of clothing. If God takes care of these things for lesser creatures like birds and flowers, won't he care for those needs for his greater creatures, those of us who love him and worship him?

What drives the point home is that Jesus does not say that the birds have a heavenly Father. That is true only of those of us who are his children by faith. If the Creator cares for his creatures, we can be even more certain that the Father will look after his children.

More Thoughts on Worry

MATTHEW 6:31-34

> [31]So do not worry, saying, "What shall we eat?" or "What shall we drink?" or "What shall we wear?" [32]For the pagans run after all these things, and your heavenly Father knows that you need them. [33]But seek first his kingdom and his righteousness, and all these things will be given to you as well. [34]Therefore do not worry about tomorrow, for tomorrow will worry about itself. Each day has enough trouble of its own.

Jesus devotes more words to the subject of worry than he does to any other issue in Matthew 6. He has already made the point that worry is inconsistent with confident faith in the Father's care; now he wants us to realize that worry is a waste—a waste of time, a waste of thought and a waste of energy. We really do need to live a day at a time. We should plan for the future, of course, but not worry about the future. One day's trouble is enough for one day. So why do we focus so much on the day we can do nothing about?

Jesus mentions two days, today and tomorrow. All worry is about *tomorrow*, whether we worry about food or clothing or a new job or anything else, but all worry is experienced *today*! Worry focuses our fear on the future and at the same time robs us of the joy of the present.

Jesus is certainly not promoting laziness—just sitting back in an easy chair and muttering, "God will provide." We have to work. The apostle Paul said, "The one who is unwilling to work shall not eat" (2 Thessalonians 3:10). God provides by giving us the opportunity to work and to earn money to buy life's necessities: food, clothing, drink and all the rest. So then God's children are not promised freedom from work, nor the freedom from the responsibility to care for others in need, and certainly not freedom from the troubles and cares of life. We are only promised freedom from worry. Jesus doesn't just make a polite suggestion in these verses; he makes it a command—"So do not worry."

God's Rule and God's Righteousness

MATTHEW 6:33

> ³³But seek first his kingdom and his righteousness, and all these things will be given to you as well.

The ambition of people outside of the Christian faith focuses on material goals—a better car, a larger house, greater fame, greater acclaim. But this ambition cannot be right for a Christian, partly because "your heavenly Father knows that you need them," but mostly because these things are not a worthy goal for the Christian's desire. The follower of Jesus must have something else, something higher that they will seek—not material things but spiritual values; not our own good but God's good; in fact, not food and clothing, but the kingdom and the righteousness of God.

When Jesus speaks of the kingdom of God, he is not referring to God's general sovereign reign over history and nature, but to his specific rule over his own people, which begins in our lives when we repent and submit and believe. God's kingdom is Jesus ruling over his people. To "seek first" this kingdom is to desire of first importance the spread of the reign of Jesus Christ—in our own lives, in our circle of acquaintances and in the global witness of the church.

God's righteousness is a wider concept than God's kingdom. It includes individual and social righteousness. God, because he is a righteous God, desires right living in every human community, not just in the church. One of God's purposes for his new and redeemed community is to make his righteousness attractive through them.

How do we make it our ambition to seek first God's kingdom and his righteousness? Everyone is ambitious, but ultimately there are only two possible ambitions for human beings—the self-centered and the God-centered. We can be ambitious either for ourselves or for God. Ambitions for ourselves may be modest or grand, but they all center around us—our comfort, our wealth, our status, our influence. Ambitions for God, however, can never be small or modest. How can we ever be content that he should acquire just a little more honor in the world? Once we are convinced that God is King, then we long to see him crowned with glory and honor and given the supreme place in people's hearts. We become ambitious for the spread of his kingdom and righteousness everywhere.

When this is genuinely our ambition, then two things occur. First, all our material needs will be provided. That's what Jesus said, "all these things will be given to you as well." But second, there will be no harm in pursuing secondary ambitions since these will be placed under our primary ambition. Christians should be eager to develop their gifts, to widen their opportunities, to extend their influence, to succeed in their careers. This ambition is not to boost their own ego or to build their own empire, but through these ambitions to bring glory to God.

Matthew 6:19-34

....

DISCUSSION GUIDE

OPEN

What are your goals and ambitions in life? Which one is your top priority?

STUDY

Read Matthew 6:19-34.

1. What do you think Jesus means by "treasures in heaven" in verse 20?

2. What makes "treasures in heaven" different from "treasures on earth"?

3. How would you explain verse 21 ("For where your treasure is, there your heart will be also") to a friend or coworker?

4. Jesus counsels us to be "full of light" in verse 22. What things distort your vision of life and your value before God?

5. List the reasons Jesus gives for *not* being preoccupied with food and clothing in verses 25-34.

6. What do these verses suggest you can do to lower your worry level about material things?

7. Jesus contrasts the ambitions of the world ("the pagans" [v. 32]) with what his disciples should seek after (v. 33). How does Jesus teaching fit with the ambitions you listed for your own life?

APPLY

1. What do you see as "money" or "wealth" in your life—the thing that has the potential to be your master?

2. How do you intentionally seek first the kingdom of God and his righteousness?

3. What would need to change in your life tomorrow if you took this command more seriously than you do right now?

4. Spend some time thinking and praying about your goals in life. What would it mean to place them on the altar of the lordship of Christ and let him change them as he desires?

- "Father - Does my heart delight in the ways of you, or this world?"
- what are the signs that something is competing for the central allegience and priority of your life?

7

Matthew 7:1-12
A Christian's Relationships

❦

Toward Our Brother or Sister

MATTHEW 7:1-2

[1]Do not judge, or you too will be judged. [2]For in the same way you judge others, you will be judged, and with the measure you use, it will be measured to you.

The connecting thread that runs through Matthew 7 is relationships. Jesus has talked about a Christian's character, influence, righteousness, religious practice and ambition, so it's not surprising that Jesus now focuses on relationships within the believing community and between Christians and unbelievers. He begins with our attitude toward brothers and sisters in Christ.

Jesus does not expect the Christian community to be perfect. He realizes that there will be misunderstandings and problems. In particular, Jesus focuses on how Christians are to relate to each other when one of them misbehaves. What kind of correction should take place in the family of believers? Jesus' instructions are well-known but often misunderstood—"Do not judge, or you too will be judged."

Jesus is *not* saying that we are to suspend any moral judgment in regard to other people, that we are to turn a blind eye to their faults and refuse to discern between truth and error or between good behavior and sinful behavior. Many times Jesus passed moral judgment on the actions of others, and just as many times in Scripture we are challenged to test all things by the standard of God's Word. This very command not to judge others is followed almost immediately by two further commands: to avoid giving what is holy to dogs or pearls to pigs, and to watch for false prophets (Matthew 7:6, 15). It would be impossible to obey either of these commands without using our critical judgment. The command not to judge is not a requirement to be blind to evil or wrong. What Jesus refuses to tolerate here is not judgment but judgmentalism—that is being a critic, someone who is bent on harsh judgment, not on mercy or grace or love.

Not only are we not the judge, but we are among the judged and will be judged with greater strictness ourselves if we dare to judge others. The rationale should be clear. If we pose as judges, we cannot plead ignorance of the law we claim to be able to administer. If we enjoy occupying the bench, we must not be surprised to find ourselves on trial.

The critic is a fault finder who is negative and destructive toward other people, and who enjoys actively seeking out their failures. Critical, judgmental people set themselves up in the place of God, but no human being is qualified to be that kind of judge. Only God can read human hearts or see the hidden motives.

Removing the Speck; Blinded by the Plank

MATTHEW 7:3-5

> [3]Why do you look at the speck of sawdust in your brother's eye and pay no attention to the plank in your own eye? [4]How can you say to your brother, "Let me take the speck out of your eye," when all the time there is a plank in your own eye? [5]You hypocrite, first take the plank out of your own eye, and then you will see clearly to remove the speck from your brother's eye.

Not only are we unfit to sit in judgment and condemn another Christian because we are *fallible* human beings, but because we are also *fallen* human beings. So we are in no position to stand in judgment on our fellow sinners.

Jesus points out this problem in a strikingly humorous way. Picture someone struggling with the delicate removal of a speck of sawdust from a friend's eye, while a long plank of wood in his own eye entirely blocks his vision. We have a tendency to exaggerate the faults and failures of others while we minimize the seriousness of our own faults and failures.

We seem to find it impossible to be strictly objective and impartial when comparing ourselves with others. On the contrary, we have a rosy view of ourselves and a skeptical view of others. Indeed, we often see our own faults in others and judge them vicariously. That way, we experience the pleasure of self-righteousness without the pain of penitence. This kind of hypocrisy is more unpleasant because an apparent act of kindness (taking a speck of dirt from somebody's eye) is made the means of inflating our own ego.

Spirit of comparison leads to judgement!

Our Christian duty, then, is not to point out the speck in our brother's eye, nor is it to try to remove the speck with a plank sticking out of our own eye. Jesus says to first remove the plank from our own eye—first deal with the sins in our own lives—and then we will have the clear vision needed to be able to take the speck out of our brother or sister's eye. We need to be as critical of ourselves as we are of others, and as generous to others as we always are to ourselves.

Dealing with the Dogs

Matthew 7:6

> [6]Do not give dogs what is sacred; do not throw your pearls
> to pigs. If you do, they may trample them under their feet,
> and turn and tear you to pieces.

The minute Jesus tells us not to judge, he also tells us that certain human beings can act like animals and may accurately be called dogs and pigs! At first sight and hearing this is startling language from the lips of Jesus, especially in the Sermon on the Mount, and especially coming immediately after his appeal for constructive Christian behavior. But Jesus always called a spade a spade. The context provides a healthy balance. If we are not to judge others, finding fault with them in a censorious, condemning or hypocritical way, we are not to ignore their faults either and pretend that everybody is the same. Both extremes are to be avoided. The saints are not judges, but, as Spurgeon said, "saints are not simpletons" either.

By giving people these names Jesus is indicating that they are like animals with some filthy habits. The dogs Jesus had in mind were not the cute lap dogs of an elegant home but the wild scavenger dogs that prowled through the city's garbage dumps. Pigs loved to wallow in mud and were unclean animals to the Jews. His command is that we should "not give dogs what is sacred" and not throw "pearls to pigs." A Jewish person (the original listeners to this Sermon) would never offer food that came from a temple sacrifice (sacred food) to a dog. They would never dream of taking expensive pearls and throwing them into a pigpen. The pigs would try to eat the pearls and, finding them inedible, would simply trample them into the mud and maybe even turn to attack the person who offered the pearls to them.

The best explanation of Jesus' teaching is to link the pearls to the pearl "of great value" in a later parable where the pearl represents the kingdom of God or salvation, and by extension the message of the gospel (Matthew 13:46). Jesus wasn't forbidding us from sharing the gospel with unbelievers since the whole thrust of Jesus' parting command in the Gospel of Matthew is to "make disciples of all nations" (Matthew 28:19). So these are not just regular unbelievers Jesus is talking about but those people who have had abundant opportunity to hear and to receive the message of the gospel, but have decisively and even defiantly rejected it.

Our Christian witness is to be conducted with discernment. If people have had plenty of opportunity to hear the truth but refuse to respond to it, if they stubbornly turn their backs on Christ, if they present themselves as dogs and pigs, we are not to go on and on with them. If we do, we cheapen God's gospel by letting them trample it under foot. Can anything be more self-condemning than to mistake God's precious pearl for a thing of no worth and to push it into the mud? At the same time, to give up on people is a very serious step to take. This teaching of Jesus is for exceptional situations only. Our normal Christian response is to be patient and persevere with others, as God has patiently persevered with us.

Our Attitude Toward Our Heavenly Father

MATTHEW 7:7-11

> [7]Ask and it will be given to you; seek and you will find; knock and the door will be opened to you. [8]For everyone who asks receives; the one who seeks finds; and to the one who knocks, the door will be opened.
>
> [9]Which of you, if your son asks for bread, will give him a stone? [10]Or if he asks for a fish, will give him a snake? [11]If you, then, though you are evil, know how to give good gifts to your children, how much more will your Father in heaven give good gifts to those who ask him!

This passage is not the first instruction on prayer in the Sermon on the Mount. Jesus has already warned us against hypocrisy and endless repetition, and has given us his own model prayer. Now, however, he actively encourages us to persevere in prayer by giving us some very gracious promises. Jesus impresses his promises on our mind and memory by the hammer blows of repetition: "Ask . . . seek . . . knock." Then, the promises are expressed in the broadest statements: "For everyone who asks receives; the one who seeks finds; and to the one who knocks, the door will be opened."

If that isn't enough to make his teaching memorable, Jesus illustrates the promises with a parable. He pictures a situation that all his hearers will find familiar—a child coming to their parent with a request. If the child asks for bread, will that child be given something that looks a bit like bread but is in fact disastrously different—a stone instead of bread or a snake instead of a fish? Of course not! Even though parents are evil (fallen in sin and selfish by nature), they still love their children and give them only good gifts. Jesus' argument is this: If fallen and self-centered human parents know how to give good things to their children, how much more will our heavenly Father (who is not evil or selfish) give good things to those who ask him?

What could be simpler than this concept of prayer? If we belong to Christ, God is our Father, we are his children, and prayer is coming to him with our requests. The trouble is that for many of us this seems too simple. We are too sophisticated to accept such a humble, childlike approach to prayer, and so our prayers go unanswered because we never ask.

What prayers have gone unanswered b/c we never ask?

Prayer Promises or Prayer Problems?

MATTHEW 7:7-8

> [7]Ask and it will be given to you; seek and you will find; knock and the door will be opened to you. [8]For everyone who asks receives; the one who seeks finds; and to the one who knocks, the door will be opened.

This passage opens the door to the problem of unanswered prayer. Jesus says, "Ask," and so we ask, fervently and in faith, but God does not give us what we ask for. We've probably all heard a person say something like "I asked to be healed (or to pass an exam or to get a new job) and, instead of receiving the blessing, things got worse. Prayer doesn't work!"

The best way to approach this issue is to remember that the promises of Jesus in the Sermon on the Mount are not unconditional. "Ask and it will be given to you" is not an absolute pledge with no strings attached. Prayer is not waving a magic wand that allows any wish to be granted and every dream to come true. That would turn God into our servant who appears instantly to do whatever we want at the moment.

Maybe we could explain these promises this way: being *good*, our heavenly Father gives only good gifts to his children; being *wise* as well, he knows which gifts are good and which are not. We have already heard Jesus say that human parents would never give a stone or snake to their children who ask for bread or fish. But what if a child through ignorance or in a fit of temper were actually to ask for a stone to bite on or a poisonous snake to play with? What would even the most accommodating parent do in that situation? A parent who is good and wise would absolutely refuse that request. Certainly our heavenly Father would never give us something harmful, even if we asked for it urgently and repeatedly, for the simple reason that he gives his children only good gifts.

So then if we ask for good things, he gives them; if we ask for things that are not good (either not good in themselves or not good for us or for others, now or in the future) he denies them,

What about praying for someone to come to the Lord? what about that going unanswered?

and only he knows the difference. That leads us to thank God for his answers to our prayers—his answers of yes and his answers of no. Both answers are good gifts from his hand.

Our Attitude Toward Others

MATTHEW 7:12

> [12] So in everything, do to others what you would have them do to you, for this sums up the Law and the Prophets.

Much has been written about the observation that Jesus' Golden Rule is found in a similar—but always negative—form in other places. Confucius, for example is credited with saying "Do not to others what you would not wish done to yourself." In the books of the Apocrypha we find "Do not do to anyone what you yourself would hate" (Tobit 4:15 NEB). The famous Jewish rabbi Hillel was asked by a student to teach him the whole law while standing on one foot. Rabbi Hillel said, "What is hateful to you, do not do to anyone else. This is the whole law; all the rest is only commentary" (Talmud *Sabbat* 31a).

There is really an enormous difference between the negative and rather grudging statement of Hillel and the positive initiative contained in Jesus' instruction: "Do to others what you would have them do to you." It may sound a rather low standard, like "Love your neighbor as yourself." But it is a remarkably flexible ethical principle. Self-advantage often guides us in our own affairs; now we must also let it guide us in our behavior to others.

All we have to do is use our imagination, put ourselves in the other person's shoes and ask, "How would I like to be treated in this situation?" This covers a wide spectrum of situations without requiring long lists of rules for each case. In fact, it is a principle of such wide application that Jesus could add "for this sums up the Law and the Prophets." Whoever directs their conduct toward others according to how they would like others to treat them in the same situation has fulfilled the admonitions of the Law and the Prophets, at least in the matter of neighbor love.

The Golden Rule will transform our actions. If we put ourselves sensitively in the place of the other person, and wish for that person what we would wish for ourselves, we would never be mean but always generous; never harsh but always understanding; never cruel but always kind.

if you've read this before, is there anything that stuck out to you that has been different?

Matthew 7:1-12

....

Discussion Guide

Open

Think of a time when you have been judged in a critical, negative way by another Christian. What did it feel like?

Now can you recall a time when you criticized someone else? How do you suppose that person felt?

Study

Read Matthew 7:1-12.

1. What does Jesus warn will be the consequences of being a critical, judgmental person?

2. How would you tell the parable of the speck and the plank to someone else in your own words?

3. What does Jesus say is the solution to such a problem?

4. Who do you think Jesus is referring to when he talks about dogs and pigs?

5. What should be your response to someone who despises and insults the message of the gospel?

6. How would you answer a person who says that they prayed and asked God for something just like Jesus instructs, but their prayer was never answered?

7. What would you say to a person who sees these statements on prayer as a guarantee that God is obligated to give us whatever we ask for if we have enough faith?

8. How does Jesus' teaching on prayer help you grow in your prayer life?

9. Is living by the Golden Rule enough to get a person into heaven? Why or why not?

APPLY

1. In what areas do you tend to be most judgmental toward other people?

2. How can you begin to allow the Holy Spirit to change your attitude in those areas?

3. What can you do to make sure that the "planks" in your own eye are removed and taken out of the way?

4. Is there someone this week you have treated in a way that you would not want to be treated? How might you apologize or make amends with that person?

other:
- Do you find it easier to judge others or yourself?

8

Matthew 7:13-29
A Christian's Commitment

❦

The Essential Choice

MATTHEW 7:13-14

¹³Enter through the narrow gate. For wide is the gate and broad is the road that leads to destruction, and many enter through it. ¹⁴But small is the gate and narrow the road that leads to life, and only a few find it.

Jesus brings his sermon to a close by confronting his hearers with the absolute necessity of a choice. The contrast between the two kinds of righteousness, the two treasures, the two masters and the two ambitions has been faithfully presented; now the time for a decision has come. Jesus insists that ultimately there is only one choice to make, because there are only two possibilities to choose from.

First, there are two ways. One way is easy and wide. There is plenty of room on this road for diversity of opinion and a whole range of personal practices. It is the road of tolerance and permissiveness. It has no curbs, no boundaries of thought or conduct. Travelers on the road follow their own desires. The hard way, on the other hand, is narrow. Its boundaries are clearly marked. Its narrowness is defined by what God has revealed in Scripture to be true and good.

Second, there are two gates. The gate leading to the easy way is wide. There is no limit to the luggage we can take with us. We don't need to leave anything behind, not even our sin or pride. The gate leading to the hard way, however, is narrow. We have to look for it to find it. It is easy to miss, and in order to enter it we have to leave everything behind—sin, selfish ambition, even family and friends at times. The narrow gate is entered one person at a time. The gate is Jesus himself. "I am the gate," he said, "whoever enters through me will be saved" (John 10:9).

There are also two destinations. Jesus taught that the easy way, entered by the wide gate, leads to destruction. He did not define what he meant by this, but the prospect is too awful to contemplate without tears. For the broad road is suicide road. By contrast, the hard way, entered by the narrow gate, leads to life—eternal life, which Jesus explained in terms of present and eternal fellowship with God. It begins here but is perfected hereafter, when we see and share his glory, and find perfect fulfillment as human beings in the selfless service of him and of our fellows.

Fourth, there are two crowds. Entering by the wide gate and traveling along the easy road to destruction are many. The narrow and hard way that leads to life, however, seems to be comparatively deserted—"only a few find it." Jesus seems to have anticipated that his followers would be a minority movement. He saw multitudes on the broad road, laughing and carefree with apparently no thought for the dreadful end ahead of them, while on the narrow road there is just a small band of pilgrims, hand in hand, backs turned from sin and faces set toward the Celestial City. None of us like to be forced to make a choice, but Jesus will not allow us to escape it.

A Warning About False Teachers

MATTHEW 7:15-20

> [15]Watch out for false prophets. They come to you in sheep's clothing, but inwardly they are ferocious wolves. [16]By their fruit you will recognize them. Do people pick grapes from thornbushes, or figs from thistles? [17]Likewise, every good tree bears good fruit, but a bad tree bears bad fruit. [18]A good tree cannot bear bad fruit, and a bad tree cannot bear good fruit. [19]Every tree that does not bear good fruit is cut down and thrown into the fire. [20]Thus, by their fruit you will recognize them.

In telling people to "watch out for false prophets," Jesus obviously assumed that such people existed. He also made the assumption that a standard of truth exists that their false teaching has departed from. In biblical terms a true prophet is one who taught God's truth by divine inspiration and insight; a false prophet claimed the same inspiration but actually spoke untruth.

Jesus made it clear that these false prophets are both dangerous and deceptive. Their danger is that in reality they are wolves. Wolves are natural enemies of sheep, and sheep have very little defense against them, but a good shepherd is responsible to protect his sheep. The deceptive work of false prophets is seen in the fact that Jesus issues his warning about them immediately after his teaching about the two ways and two destinations. False prophets are adept at blurring the truth of salvation. They distort the gospel message and make it hard for genuine seekers to find the narrow gate. Others try to convince us that the narrow way is in reality much broader than Jesus implied, or that Jesus was mistaken in his teaching and the broad road does not lead to destruction after all. In fact, they tell us, all roads lead to God—a statement that Jesus absolutely rejects!

So, "Beware!" Jesus warns. We must be on our guard, pray for discernment, use our critical faculties and never relax our vigilance. We must not be dazzled by their outward clothing—their charm or learning. We must look beneath the appearance to the reality. What lives under the fleece: a sheep or a wolf?

Jesus gives us a test for a prophet, the test of fruit. Although you may sometimes mistake a wolf for a sheep, you can't make the same mistake with a tree. No tree can hide its true identity for long. Sooner or later it betrays itself by its fruit. A wolf may disguise itself; a tree cannot. The fruit produced in a prophet's life refers to the prophet's character and conduct. If we see the fruit of the Spirit in a prophet or teacher's life—love, patience, goodness, self-control—we have reason to believe the prophet is true. If those qualities are missing, however, and the works of the flesh are more apparent—jealousy, impurity, pride—we are justified in suspecting that the prophet is an imposter.

Another test of a prophet's fruit is the actual teaching that the prophet proclaims. Is the prophet's message in accord with the original instruction from the apostles recorded in the New Testament? Does the prophet confess Jesus as the Messiah who has come in human flesh? Sound doctrine and holy living are the marks of a genuine teacher and prophet of God.

Of course the application of the fruit test is not altogether simple or straightforward. For fruit takes time to grow and ripen. We have to wait for it patiently. We also need an opportunity to examine it closely, for it is not always possible to recognize a tree and its fruit from a distance. To apply this to teachers, what is needed is not a superficial estimate of their standing in the church but a close and critical scrutiny of their character, conduct, message, motives and influence. This warning of Jesus gives us no encouragement, however, either to become suspicious of everybody or to take up as our hobby the disreputable sport known as heresy hunting. Rather it is a solemn reminder that there are false teachers in the church, and that we are to be on our guard.

Saying or Doing?

MATTHEW 7:21-23

> [21]Not everyone who says to me, "Lord, Lord," will enter the kingdom of heaven, but only the one who does the will of my Father who is in heaven. [22]Many will say to me on that day, "Lord, Lord, did we not prophesy in your name and in your name drive out demons and in your name

> perform many miracles?" [23]Then I will tell them plainly, "I never knew you. Away from me, you evildoers!"

The people Jesus has in mind here are relying for salvation on a verbal affirmation of faith but with no heart reality. They are trusting in what they *say* to Jesus or about Jesus. But our final destiny will be settled, Jesus insists, not by what we merely say to him today, nor by what we say to him at the last judgment, but by whether we do what we say, whether our verbal profession is followed by moral obedience.

Jesus is not dismissing the importance of a verbal profession of our faith and commitment to him as Lord. According to the apostle Paul, we are required to confess with our lips and believe in our hearts in order to be genuinely born again (Romans 10:9-10). The profession Jesus talks about in these verses seems on the surface to be wonderful. It is polite; it addresses Jesus as "Lord." The profession is doctrinally correct; none of the activities done in Jesus' name are outside Christian practice. Along with polite and correct, we could add that the profession is passionate; it is not cold or formal but includes an enthusiastic "Lord, Lord," as if the speaker wants to draw attention to the strength of his or her devotion. The profession these people make is not private or hidden but made in public view and in full voice. They prophesied and cast out demons and did many miraculous works. What they stress above all is the name in which they have accomplished so many wondrous things. Three times they use it, and each time they put it first for emphasis. They claim that they have done these things in the name of Christ. What better Christian profession could be made?

Jesus moves on from what these people say to him to what he will say to them. He makes a solemn profession too, but he speaks terrible words: "I never knew you. Away from me, you evildoers!"

The reason Jesus rejects them is that their profession is verbal but not heartfelt and genuine. It concerns their lips only and not their life. They call Jesus "Lord, Lord," but never have submitted to his lordship or obeyed the will of his heavenly Father.

We who claim to be Christians today have made a profession of faith in conversion and at baptism. We appear to honor Jesus by referring to him as Lord. We recite the creeds of the church and sing worship songs with outward devotion. We may even carry out a variety of ministries in his name. But Jesus is not impressed by our pious words. He still asks for evidence of our faith in works of obedience and in hearts of surrender to him.

Two Foundations

MATTHEW 7:24-27

24Therefore everyone who hears these words of mine and puts them into practice is like a wise man who built his house on the rock. 25The rain came down, the streams rose, and the winds blew and beat against that house; yet it did not fall, because it had its foundation on the rock. 26But everyone who hears these words of mine and does not put them into practice is like a foolish man who built his house on sand. 27The rain came down, the streams rose, and the winds blew and beat against that house, and it fell with a great crash.

The contrast in the previous section of the Sermon was between *saying* and *doing*; the contrast now is between *hearing* and *doing*. There is a person, Jesus says, who "hears these words of mine and puts them into practice," and there is also a person who "hears these words of mine and does not put them into practice." He then illustrates the contrast between his obedient hearers and his disobedient hearers by his parable of the two builders. The wise builder dug deep and constructed his house on bedrock; the foolish builder could not be bothered with foundations and was content to build on the sand. As both moved forward with their buildings, the casual observer would not have noticed any difference between the two structures. The difference was in the foundation, and foundations are rarely seen. Only when a storm broke were the foundational issues revealed. The house built on the rock withstood the storm, while the house on the sand collapsed in ruin.

In the same way, professing Christians (both the genuine and the false) often look alike. You cannot easily tell which is which. Both appear to be building Christian lives. Jesus is not contrasting a professing Christian with an unbeliever in this parable, but two professing believers. They both hear Jesus' words. Both are members of the visible Christian community. Both read the Bible, go to church and listen to sermons. The reason you cannot tell the difference between them is that the deep foundations of their lives are hidden from view. The real question is not whether they *hear* Christ's teaching but whether they *do* what they hear. Only a storm will reveal the truth. It may be a storm of crisis or calamity that uncovers the genuineness or falseness of their claim to faith. If not, certainly the storm of the day of judgment will reveal all that is hidden.

The Path of Obedience

MATTHEW 7:24

²⁴Therefore everyone who hears these words of mine and puts them into practice is like a wise man who built his house on the rock.

The truth that Jesus has been pressing home in these final two paragraphs of the Sermon is that neither an abundance of biblical knowledge nor a verbal profession of faith (though both are essential in themselves) can ever be a substitute for obedience to Jesus. The question is not whether we *say* nice, polite, correct, enthusiastic things to or about Jesus; nor whether we *hear* his words, listening, studying, pondering and memorizing until our minds are stuffed with his teaching; but whether we *do* what we say and *do* what we know, in other words whether the lordship of Jesus is our life's central reality.

This is not, of course, to teach that the way of salvation is by good works of obedience. The whole New Testament offers salvation only by the grace of God through faith apart from our works. What Jesus is stressing, however, is that those who truly hear the gospel and profess faith will give evidence of that faith by the obedience of their lives.

In applying Jesus' teaching to ourselves, we need to consider that the Bible is a dangerous book to read, and that the church is a dangerous society to join. In reading the Bible we hear the words of Christ, and in joining the church we say we believe in Christ. As a result, we belong to the company described by Jesus as both hearing his teaching and calling him Lord. Our membership therefore lays on us the serious responsibility of being sure that what we know and what we say are translated into what we do.

Who Is This Preacher?

MATTHEW 7:28-29

> [28]When Jesus had finished saying these things, the crowds were amazed at his teaching, [29]because he taught as one who had authority, and not as their teachers of the law.

Many people—including adherents of other religions and of none—tell us that they are prepared to accept the Sermon on the Mount as the essence of Jesus' teaching. Here, they say, is Jesus of Nazareth, the moral teacher, at his simplest and best. Here is the core of his message before it became encrusted with the additions of his interpreters. Here is the "original Jesus," with plain talk and no church dogma, an unsophisticated preacher of righteousness, claiming to be no more than a human teacher, and telling us to do good and to love one another.

But this popular explanation of the Sermon cannot stand up to serious examination. Under closer inspection we find that it is impossible to drive a wedge between the Jesus of the Sermon on the Mount and the Jesus of the rest of the New Testament. The preacher of the Sermon is the same supernatural, outspoken, divine Jesus who is to be found everywhere else. So the main question the Sermon forces on us is not so much "What do you make of this teaching?" as "Who on earth is this teacher?"

What struck the first hearers of the Sermon was the preacher's extraordinary authority. He did not stumble or hesitate. Instead, with quiet assurance he laid down the law for the citizens of God's kingdom. And the crowds were amazed—and after two thousand years, we are amazed too! Jesus teaches with the authority of God. He expects people to build the structure of their lives on his words and adds that only those who do so are wise. He says he has come to fulfill the Law and the Prophets. He is both the Lord to be obeyed and the Savior who brings eternal blessings. He casts himself in the central role of the drama of the final judgment. He speaks of God as his Father in a unique sense, and implies that what he does God does. How can such a teacher be written off as simply one more in a long line of merely human religious leaders?

Christians take Jesus at his word and his claims at face value. We respond to his Sermon with complete seriousness. Here is Jesus' picture of his alternative society. These are the standards, the values and the priorities of the kingdom of God. Too often the church has turned away from this challenge and sunk into a bourgeois, conformist respectability. At such times it is almost indistinguishable from the world, it has lost its saltiness, its light is extinguished, and it repels all idealists. For it gives no evidence that it is God's new society that is tasting already the joys and powers of the age to come. Only when the Christian community lives by Christ's manifesto will the world be attracted and God be glorified. So when Jesus calls us to himself, it is to this that he calls us. For he is the Lord of the counterculture.

Matthew 7:13-29

....

Discussion Guide

OPEN

Think of a recent decision you had to make. How many alternatives did you have?

How do you respond when a choice has to be made?

STUDY

Read Matthew 7:13–29.

1. What is attractive and appealing about the broad way Jesus describes in verses 13-14?

2. What is unappealing about the narrow way?

3. What is the fundamental difference between the two ways?

4. To what extent have you found what Jesus says about the two ways to be true in your experience?

5. Why are false prophets so dangerous?

6. Do you think the "fruit" test is a valid one?

7. How would you explain that test to a new Christian?

8. What surprises you about those who do great things in Jesus' name but who are ultimately rejected by Jesus (vv. 21-23)?

9. Would you have come to the same conclusion Jesus came to simply by your own observation?

10. What is the danger of Christians hearing Jesus' words but not putting them into practice?

11. Do you agree that "the Bible is a dangerous book to read" and "the church is a dangerous society to join"? Explain your answer.

12. How would you answer someone who said that they just wanted to follow the simple Jesus of the Sermon on the Mount?

APPLY

1. How can you strengthen the obedience factor in your life?

2. How would you discern whether a prophet or teacher was genuinely from God or was false?

3. Which of the teachings of Jesus in the Sermon on the Mount has touched you most deeply?

4. Pray that you might align your life more closely with Jesus' teaching in the Sermon.

Guidelines for Leaders

My grace is sufficient for you.

2 CORINTHIANS 12:9

If leading a small group is something new for you, don't worry. These sessions are designed to flow naturally and be led easily. You may even find that the studies seem to lead themselves!

This study guide is flexible. You can use it with a variety of groups—students, professionals, coworkers, friends, neighborhood or church groups. Each study takes forty-five to sixty minutes in a group setting.

You don't need to be an expert on the Bible or a trained teacher to lead a small group. These guides are designed to facilitate a group's discussion, not a leader's presentation. Guiding group members to discover together what the Bible has to say and to listen together for God's guidance will help them remember much more than a lecture would.

There are some important facts to know about group dynamics and encouraging discussion. The suggestions that follow should equip you to effectively and enjoyably fulfill your role as leader.

Preparing for the Study

1. Ask God to help you understand and apply the passage in your own life. Unless this happens, you will not be prepared to lead others. Pray too for the various members of the group. Ask God to open your hearts to the message of his Word and motivate you to action.

2. Read the introduction to the entire guide to get an overview of the topics that will be explored. *The Message of the Sermon on the Mount* will give you more detailed information on the text. This can help you deal with answers to tough questions about the text and its context that could come up in discussion.

3. As you begin each study, read and reread the assigned Bible passage to familiarize yourself with it.

4. Carefully work through each question in the study. Spend time in meditation and reflection as you consider how to respond.

5. Write your thoughts and responses. This will help you express your understanding of the passage clearly.

6. It may help to have a Bible dictionary handy. Use it to look up any unfamiliar words, names or places.

7. Reflect seriously on how you need to apply the Scripture to your life. Remember that the group members will follow

your lead in responding to the studies. They will not go any deeper than you do.

LEADING THE STUDY

1. At the beginning of your first time together, explain that these studies are meant to be discussions, not lectures. Encourage the members of the group to participate. However, do not put pressure on those who may be hesitant to speak—especially during the first few sessions.

2. Be sure that everyone in your group has a book. Encourage the group to prepare beforehand for each discussion by reading the introduction to the book and the readings for each section.

3. Begin each study on time. Open with prayer, asking God to help the group to understand and apply the passage.

4. Discuss the "Open" question before the Bible passage is read. The "Open" question introduces the theme of the study and helps group members begin to open up, and can reveal where our thoughts and feelings need to be transformed by Scripture. Reading the passage first could tend to color the honest reactions people might otherwise give—because they are, of course, supposed to think the way the Bible does. Encourage as many members as possible to respond to the "Open" question, and be ready to get the discussion going with your own response.

5. Have a group member read aloud the passage to be studied as indicated in the guide.

6. The study questions are designed to be read aloud just as they are written. You may, however, prefer to express them in your own words. There may be times when it is appropriate to deviate from the discussion guide. For example, a question may have already been answered. If so, move on to the next question. Or someone may raise an important question not covered in the guide. Take time to discuss it, but try to keep the group from going off on tangents.

7. Avoid answering your own questions. An eager group quickly becomes passive and silent if members think the leader will do most of the talking. If necessary, repeat or rephrase the question until it is clearly understood, or refer to the commentary woven into the guide to clarify the context or meaning.

8. Don't be afraid of silence in response to the discussion questions. People may need time to think about the question before formulating their answers.

9. Don't be content with just one answer. Ask, "What do the rest of you think?" or "Anything else?" until several people have given answers to the question.

10. Try to be affirming whenever possible. Affirm participation. Never reject an answer; if it is clearly off base, ask, "Which verse led you to that conclusion?" or again, "What do the rest of you think?"

11. Don't expect every answer to be addressed to you, even though this will probably happen at first. As group members

become more at ease, they will begin to truly interact with each other. This is one sign of healthy discussion.

12. Don't be afraid of controversy. It can be very stimulating. If you don't resolve an issue completely, don't be frustrated. Explain that the group will move on and God may enlighten all of you in later sessions.

13. Periodically summarize what the group has said about the passage. This helps to draw together the various ideas mentioned and gives continuity to the study. But don't preach.

14. Conclude your time together with prayer, asking for God's help in following through on the applications you've identified.

15. End on time.

Many more suggestions and helps for studying a passage or guiding discussion can be found in *How to Lead a LifeGuide Bible Study* and *The Big Book on Small Groups* (both from InterVarsity Press).

Reading the Bible with John Stott

- *Reading the Sermon on the Mount with John Stott*

- *Reading Romans with John Stott, volume 1*

- *Reading Romans with John Stott, volume 2*

- *Reading Galatians with John Stott*

- *Reading Ephesians with John Stott*

- *Reading Timothy and Titus with John Stott*

ALSO AVAILABLE

JOHN R. W. STOTT

The Message of the
Sermon on the Mount

Revised Edition

JOHN R. W. STOTT

*The Message of the
Sermon on the Mount*
978-0-8308-2423-6